the bread book

Dedication
For my young son William who is just
discovering the joys of bread making

First published in Great Britain in 2003 by
Hamlyn, a division of Octopus Publishing Group Ltd

This edition published in 2005 by Bounty Books,
a division of Octopus Publishing Group Ltd
2–4 Heron Quays, London E14 4JP
www.octopusbooks.co.uk
Reprinted 2006, (twice), 2007, 2009

ISBN: 978-0-753713-16-7

A CIP catalogue record for this book is available from the
British Library

Printed and bound in China

the bread book

the definitive guide to making bread by hand or machine

Bounty
BOOKS

Notes

This book includes dishes made with nuts and nut derivatives. It is advisable for those with known allergic reactions to nuts and nut derivatives and those who may be potentially vulnerable to these allergies, such as pregnant and nursing mothers, invalids, the elderly, babies and children, to avoid dishes made with nuts and nut oils. It is also prudent to check the labels of preprepared ingredients for the possible inclusion of nut derivatives.

Medium eggs have been used throughout.

A range of bread making machines were used for the testing of these recipes. As machines vary considerably in size, length and type of programme, refer back to your manual and adjust the ingredient amounts, the order in which ingredients are added or change to a different programme if the manual suggests otherwise.

NOTES FOR AMERICAN READERS

UK	US
bicarbonate of soda	baking soda
caster sugar	superfine sugar
chilli seeds	crushed red pepper
clear/thick set honey	honey
coarse strong wholemeal flour	whole wheat flour
coriander	cilantro
courgettes	zucchini
dark muscovado sugar	dark brown sugar
dessert apple	sweet apple
dried chilli flakes	crushed red pepper
fast-action dried yeast	active dry yeast
flaked almonds	sliced almonds
glacé ginger	candied ginger
golden syrup	golden syrup (if unavailable, use corn syrup)
granary flour	granary flour (if unavailable, use a mixture of two-thirds whole wheat to one-third bread flour, plus a small amount of malt powder)
Greek yogurt	Greek yogurt (if unavailable, use whole milk yogurt)
icing sugar	confectioner's sugar
linseeds	flaxseeds
millet flakes	use wheat germ instead
mixed groats	buckwheat groats or kasha
molasses sugar	dark brown sugar
natural yogurt	plain yogurt
pepper (red, green or yellow)	bell pepper
plain flour	all-purpose flour
salt flakes	Kosher salt
self-raising flour	self-rising flour
soft light brown sugar	brown sugar
soft brown sugar	brown sugar
soured cream	sour cream
spring onions	scallions
strong coarse brown flour	whole wheat flour
strong white flour	bread flour
strong wholemeal flour	whole wheat flour
sultanas	golden raisins
sweetcorn	corn
treacle	molasses

contents

Introduction

Anyone can make bread – it is no longer the domain of experienced cooks or master bakers. Fast-action dried yeast has made baking with yeast child's play; simply take a pack out of the cupboard, stir it in to the flour, add warm water and away you go.

My own first attempts at a wholemeal loaf as a child left something to be desired. But spurred on with some helpful tips from a very kind baker, who gave me some specially-marked tins that I still treasure, my love of breadmaking has grown. My small son now makes bread with me, his kneading is rather more boisterous and exuberant than mine, but both ways get good results. Waiting and watching the dough rise is magical and a good way to encourage all the family to be interested in cooking.

For those who are really short of time, a bread machine will effortlessly and efficiently mix, knead, rise and bake your bread. All you need to do is measure out the ingredients, turn it on and walk away. Your nose will soon lead you back to the kitchen as baking begins. What could be nicer than programming a loaf to start baking when you are still in bed! When you do have more time, it can be fun and rewarding to make dough in the bread machine and then shape it by hand into a plait, ring, twist or into tiny shaped rolls.

With over 75 recipes to choose from, there is something for everyone in this book, from quick everyday breads to make and bake in a bread machine, to rustic-looking breads, hand shaped to tear and share for an informal lunch of salad or soup. Sweet breads are lovely for both leisurely breakfasts and for welcoming home hungry school children. For those who are unable to eat wheat flours, there is a section of sweet and savoury gluten-free breads too.

Whichever recipe you choose to make, one thing is true, the better the ingredients you use, the better the finished loaf will be, plus there will be none of the extra additives that manufacturers add to prolong the shelf life of shop-bought bread, so making your own bread is healthy too.

Europeans have long appreciated the value of bread and wouldn't dream of serving a meal without having it on the table. Forget about plain white bread, the types, shapes and flavours of bread are infinite: from breads made with different grains to those flavoured with carrots, pumpkin or courgette and from breads speckled with tiny seeds and chopped nuts to savoury and sweet spice combinations that are sweetened with maple syrup, honey and malt extract. What else could add so much variety to our everyday meals?

Making and baking bread by hand or in a machine is immensely satisfying and relaxing, and with the stresses of modern living, that must surely be a good thing.

Basic ingredients

The key to successful breadmaking lies in understanding your ingredients and how they react together.

FLOURS
White flours

Choose strong white flour, sometimes known as bread flour for breadmaking. This has a higher gluten content for added stretch and is recommended for use either in a bread machine or making bread by hand. Small amounts of French plain flour may be added to strong white flour to make crustier more authentic French bread. Use plain flour or self-raising flour in yeast-free breads only. If you are trying to avoid additives then choose organic, unbleached strong white flour.

Wholewheat or wholemeal flour

Milled from the whole wheat kernel it contains the bran and wheat germ making it more nutritious and giving it a nuttier flavour and coarser texture. Again, choose wholemeal flour marked 'strong', or 'bread', flour for breadmaking. Loaves made with this are denser and heavier as the bran inhibits the release of gluten, so making them take longer to rise. Compensate for this by mixing half wholewheat flour with half strong white flour for a lighter finished bread. Small amounts of wheat germ may be added to white breads if preferred.

Strong brown flour

As this contains only 80–90 per cent of the wheat kernel it produces a lighter brown loaf. Make bread just with this or mix half and half with strong white flour for a lighter bread.

Granary flour

A sweet, nutty flour made with a combination of wholemeal, white and rye flours mixed with malted wheat grains. Malthouse flour is similar to granary flour.

Low-gluten flours

Rye: generally mixed with other flours as it inhibits gluten development, it has a strong distinctive flavour so even a small amount will flavour white or wholemeal flour.

Spelt flour: a slightly nutty stoneground wheat flour that is high in protein but low in gluten, making it a possible option for those who are intolerant to other wheat flours. As the gluten is reduced the bread can collapse if proved for too long so use a fastbake or quick programme if making in a bread machine and reduce the timings slightly if making by hand.

Millet flour: a pale yellow flour that is naturally sweet, rich in protein, vitamins and minerals but low in gluten. Millet grains can be used to decorate breads before baking.

Gluten-free flours

If you are following a coeliac diet then you will need to avoid all flours that contain gluten. Gluten-free flours tend to make a denser,

smaller loaf, so increase the amount of yeast slightly to make a more open texture. Either make up a blend of flours yourself or buy a bag of mixed gluten-free flours from the supermarket instead.

If you use a bread machine for wheat- and gluten-free cooking, it is vital that you take extra care when washing out the tin and kneader blade. Even the slightest trace of wheat products in the machine may cause an allergic reaction in someone who suffers with coeliac disease.

Gram flour: this yellow flour is ground from chick peas and is also sold as chick pea flour.

Quinoa flour: contains all eight amino acids which means it is a good protein booster when added with other flours.

Cornmeal flour: this bright yellow flour is ground from dried corn kernels. It is used to make quick teabreads or American-style yeast-free breads.

Potato flour: a white flour used mostly as a thickener. Adds moistness to breads when mixed with other flours.

Brown rice flour: milled from the whole rice grain. Adds a sweet nuttiness to breads but can make the texture dry.

Buckwheat flour: this grey-brown flour has a distinctive bitter earthy flavour and, although has wheat in its name, it is gluten-free.

YEAST

The most important ingredient of all. It is available in three types: fresh yeast, traditional dried yeast that requires frothing in water before use, and fast-action dried yeast, which is used in all the recipes in this book. Fast-action dried yeast is by far the easiest and most convenient to use and needs only to be stirred into the dry ingredients.

Once a sachet of yeast is opened, seal it well, store in the fridge and use within 24 hours. Yeast works through a fermentation process. As it feeds on the sugar and later the starches in the flour, it produces a gas (carbon dioxide) and it is this gas that causes the bread to rise.

SUGAR

Sugar is a vital food for the yeast and without it fermentation cannot take place. Choose from white, light brown or dark brown sugars. Or for bread with a more distinct flavour try barley malt extract, honey, maple syrup, treacle or molasses, but as these last two are so strong, use them only in tiny amounts.

In a 500 g (1 lb) loaf, just 1 teaspoon of sugar is enough to activate the yeast, but more can be added to flavour the finished bread. Larger amounts of sugar can slow down the yeast a little so you may find you

need slightly longer rising times for sweetened breads. Do not use artificial sweeteners as the yeast will not react with them properly.

SALT

Salt acts as a flavour enhancer and, like sugar, if used in large quantities can inhibit the growth of the yeast. If you need to reduce your intake of salt for dietary reasons, add extra flavourings such as herbs or spices to compensate.

WATER

There is one main difference between making bread in a bread machine and by hand: the temperature of the water. Cold water is required for a bread machine – unless a bread is being made on a rapid or fastbake programme – whereas warm water must always be used when making bread by hand. Too hot and the yeast will be killed, too cold and the yeast won't be activated. Milk may also be used for a tender crumb. Always use powdered milk in a bread machine if using the delay timer facility.

ENRICHING INGREDIENTS

Butter, oil and eggs all add richness to the finished bread, giving a softer, more tender crumb. Butter and oil also act as a preservative and keep bread fresh for longer. Breads made without butter or oil, such as French bread, must be eaten on the day they are made.

Depending on the amounts used, fermentation of the yeast may be slowed down, so allow extra time for the first and second rising or 'proving', or set to a special programme if using a bread machine. Do not use the delay timer facility if using eggs.

Using a bread machine

CHOOSING A BREAD MACHINE
Is it within your budget?
With machines ranging from budget to expensive there is a wide range to choose from. Lower- and medium-priced machines make surprisingly good loaves, so unless you plan to make bread every day, you don't need to make a big investment in a bread machine.

Does the machine make a loaf that is the right size for your needs?
If there are just two of you, then a mini baker, making 500 g (1 lb) loaves will be perfect. For family-sized meals go for a machine that will make 750 g (1½ lb) loaves or ideally one that can make this size and a larger 1 kg (2 lb) loaf too. The medium and larger tins are more versatile as you can make smaller and larger loaves, while a small tin restricts you to only ever being able to make small loaves. Most machines have rectangular tins, a few have squarer, taller tins.

Does it have a viewing window?
It is much better to look through a glass window to check on your bread's progress, than to keep lifting the lid and so lowering the temperature.

Where will you site the machine?
If work-top space is at a premium then the size of the machine is crucial. A bread machine that is out at the ready will be used more frequently than one that is kept hidden away in a cupboard.

GETTING TO KNOW YOUR MACHINE
It sounds dull but it is worth reading your bread machine manual before you start and familiarizing yourself with the programme selection, size and crust options. One click too many and your bread may take an extra hour to bake or perhaps never be baked at all! Like anything, practice makes perfect and after a couple of uses, programming your machine will seem like child's play.

Delay timer facility
Even if you are not at home or are sleeping, you can programme the machine to come on automatically. What could be nicer than coming down on a Sunday morning to the smell of freshly baked bread or getting home from work to be welcomed by that wonderful aroma? As the ingredients will be in the machine for some hours do not use fresh milk, butter, eggs or other highly perishable ingredients. This problem is usually avoided by the use of powdered milk instead of fresh milk.

It is also crucial that the salt, sugar and yeast are kept apart from each other with the yeast being put into a little dip in the centre of the flour, well out of the way of the liquid. If the yeast comes into contact with the liquid it will begin working before the other ingredients are mixed and will have lost its power by the time the machine has switched itself on. Even if you don't plan to set the delay timer facility, a timer is invaluable so that you can see how many minutes are left to run on the programme. Some of the cheaper machines do not have this, so look carefully before buying.

What's my size?
Check that the size of the finished loaf at the top of the recipe corresponds with the tin capacity of the bread machine before you begin weighing out the ingredients. If you are unsure of the size of your tin, then check in the bread machine manual or measure and fill the tin with water. As a general rule, bread machine tins come in three sizes:

500 g (1 lb) loaf with a tin capacity of 1.3 litres (2 pints)
750 g (1½ lb) loaf with a tin capacity of 2.5 litres (4½ pints)
1 kg (2 lb) loaf with a tin capacity of 3.3 litres (5¾ pints)

Remember, you can make a smaller loaf in a bigger tin, but not the other way round!

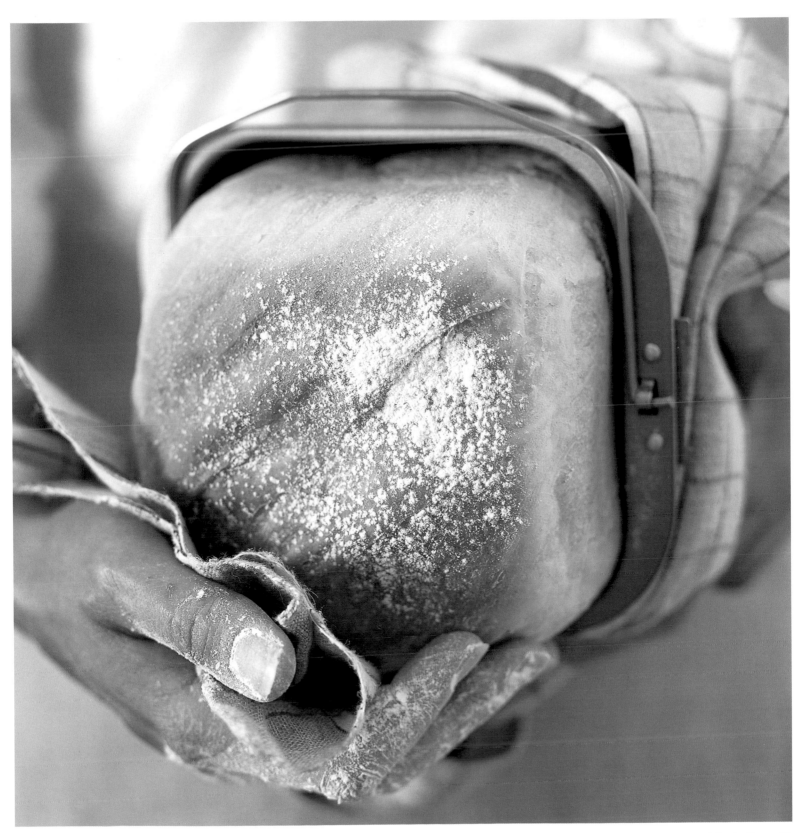

WHICH PROGRAMME TO USE?
Basic white/normal

This will probably be the most well used programme of all and will take around 2¾ hours to mix, rise and bake a good family-sized 750 g (1½ lb) loaf.

Wholewheat

This programme has a longer preheat time to allow the grain to soak up the water and expand, so making a brown loaf that is as light as possible. Making a wholewheat loaf may take 1–1½ hours longer than a normal white loaf. Some programmes even allow three risings to lighten the bread.

Rapid or fastbake

This speedy programme will make and rise a loaf in under 1 hour. To get the best results always use lukewarm water or milk to activate the yeast quickly and increase the amount of yeast used. The texture of these loaves can be a little closer and denser than other breads so use a mix of white and brown flour or all white flour for a good texture.

Sweet

As sweeter breads tend to brown more quickly, this programme ensures that they have sufficient time to rise and a lower temperature to bake in.

Cakes/quick bread

Instruction manuals vary, particularly when making cakes. Some suggest mixing the wet ingredients and dry ingredients separately then adding to the bread machine tin, while others may suggest mixing the cake completely and using the bread machine for baking only.

Generally this programme is for breads made without yeast as it does not have a rising period. The best cakes are those that are mixed and baked within 1 hour 40 minutes to 1 hour 50 minutes. If your machine takes longer than this, make sure you check on the cake's progress during baking and take it out 15 minutes or so before the end of the programme, or when cooked and golden. Otherwise, experiment and try baking the cake on the rapid or fastbake programme instead.

Dough

This programme gives you the best of both worlds. Simply put all the ingredients into the bread machine and leave it to do the mixing, kneading and rising while you get on with something else. Shape the risen dough by hand into large plaits, twists or ring loaves, tiny fancy rolls or pizza.

Accurate measuring

Measuring ingredients for a bread machine is crucial. Just a ¼ teaspoon of extra yeast could make the dough spill out of the top of the machine or cause the baked bread to stick to the roof of the machine. Make sure to use proper measuring spoons not ordinary kitchen teaspoons or serving spoons. When using a measuring jug, put it on the work surface, put your eye at the same level and check carefully that it is reading the required amount, adjust if under or over. Keep to either metric or imperial measurements and don't be tempted to use a combination of the two.

SPECIAL FEATURES

French

With more rising time, this programme produces a bread with a more open texture. Some machines also cook the bread at a higher temperature to ensure a crisp crust. Use for low-fat, low-sugar breads only.

Sandwich

A programme designed to make a light-textured bread with a softer, thicker crust.

Extra bake

This setting enables the bread machine to be used as just an oven for up to 1 hour. Or it may be used to increase the baking time on a selected or finished cycle. See your manual for more detail. You may be able to set the extra bake time in minutes or you may have to set it for the full 1 hour and turn it off manually when the time you require is up, as for the Date and Walnut Bread (see page 128).

Jam

Small quantities of jam may also be made in a breadmaker in around 1 hour using 250 g (8 oz) of stoned fruit and the same weight of preserving sugar with added pectin for a guaranteed set. Keep the kneader blade in place so that the jam is mixed as it heats.

Keep warm facility

When the bread is cooked and the set programme finished, a keep warm programme will automatically begin to keep condensation to a minimum for 30 minutes to a maximum of 1½ hours depending on size of loaf and machine. The machine will beep at regular intervals to remind you to remove the bread. If it is left in the machine after the keep warm facility has stopped then the condensation caused as the loaf cools will make the top go soggy.

Power loss memory feature

This programme is automatically activated if there is a brief power cut or the bread machine is turned off accidentally. Once power is resumed the machine will restart the interrupted programme.

Crust control

More sophisticated machines offer a choice of three crust colours: light, medium and dark. More basic machines only offer a white basic loaf and a white basic extra-baked loaf option. If your machine does not give you a choice and you would prefer a finished loaf with a darker crust, then brush the top of the bread with a little butter or egg yolk mixed with water and brown under a hot grill or put into a hot oven, 200°C (400°F), Gas Mark 6, for 5–10 minutes.

Tip Always make sure the kneader blade is removed from the base of the loaf or bottom of the bread tin after baking. If you leave it in the tin, there will be a build up of baked-on dough underneath it, making it impossible to remove and gradually causing the blade to rotate slower and slower.

Top tips

1 Check that the recipe will fit in your bread machine before you start by double checking the size of the finished loaf with your tin size and amounts of yeast and flour with your manual.

2 Be familiar with your manual, bread machines vary. While the majority suggest adding wet ingredients to the tin first, some may specify adding the flour first.

3 Take the tin out of the machine before adding the ingredients.

4 Add cold water to your bread machine tin unless using the rapid/fastbake programme.

5 Weigh ingredients carefully, the amount of fast-action dried yeast is crucial, just an extra ¼ teaspoon of yeast may be enough to make the bread dough rise right out of the machine.

6 If using perishable ingredients such as butter, eggs, milk or cheese, do not set the delay timer facility.

7 Add extra flavourings when the 'raisin beep' sounds and check that all the ingredients have mixed in. Use a plastic spatula to scrape down the sides of the tin if needed.

8 Try to resist the urge to open the lid of the bread machine when rising and baking as the cold air will slow things down.

9 Always take the tin out of the bread machine using oven gloves.

10 Take care of your bread tin and kneader blade. When removing the bread, loosen the edges with a plastic spatula so that the nonstick surface is not scratched and always clean it with warm, soapy water and a washing up brush. Check that the paddle or kneader blade is not left in the bread after baking.

Making your first loaf in a bread machine

Check your machine manual

Not all bread machines are the same so always look at your machine manual or cookbook before you try a recipe for the first time. Alter the amounts of yeast or other ingredients following machine manufacturer's directions, if necessary. You may also need to add the ingredients in the order that the manufacturers specify if different to the steps shown in this book.

Read the bread machine manual first so you are familiar with the settings and how to operate them. The many menu options available for programme, loaf and crust colour may seem a little daunting at first, but will quickly become second nature.

1 Before you begin Stand the bread machine on the work surface ensuring there is plenty of space around it for ventilation and that it is out of direct sunlight and draughts, if possible. With the bread machine unplugged, pull the bread tin (bucket) upwards and out of the machine, giving it a little twist if necessary, depending on your machine.

2 Preparing the machine Insert the paddle or kneader blade on to the spindle in the base of the tin and check that it is secure and turns easily. When your bread machine has been used a number of times, double check that there are no baked-on pieces of bread on the spindle before fitting the blade, otherwise it will not be able to rotate at the correct speed.

3 Adding wet ingredients Add the wet ingredients to the tin. Pour in the cold water or milk (unless setting to a rapid/fastbake programme where warm water is required). Beat the eggs before adding them, and then add either melted butter or butter softened to room temperature so that it mixes into the flour easily. Honey is best added at this stage too. (Do not add perishable ingredients if using the delay timer facility.)

4 Adding dry ingredients Spoon the flour over the liquid, making sure the flour covers the liquid completely, then add the dried milk powder, if using, salt, sugar, dried herbs or spices to different corners of the tin. Make a slight dip into the centre of the flour making sure that the yeast will not come into contact with the liquid. This is especially

3

3

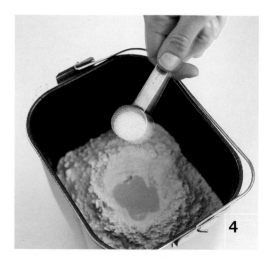

4

important if you are using the delay timer facility. Measure the yeast carefully and sprinkle it into the dip.

5 Inserting the tin into the machine Insert the tin into the bread machine carefully, lining up any arrows on the tin with any in the bread machine and making sure the tin is clicked into place securely. Shut the lid.

6 Selecting the programme Plug in the bread machine and select the programme required for the type and size of loaf being made. Some machines may also have a selection for pale, medium and dark crust too. Use the setting suggested in the recipes later on in this book, referring to your manual and adapting as necessary.

7 Starting the programme Press start. Some machines may operate a warming period while others will warm and mix immediately. Obviously those machines that mix and warm simultaneously will have shorter programme times.

8 Using the raisin beep Towards the end of the mixing stage a beep, known as the raisin beep, will sound on your machine. At this point, you can add flavourings such as dried fruit, sun-dried tomatoes or spring onions before allowing the programme to continue. Double check it after 10 minutes to make sure that the added ingredients have been fully incorporated into the dough. If not, scrape any unmixed additions down the side of tin with a plastic spatula, making sure to keep the spatula out of the way of the blade.

9 The end of the programme Close the lid and allow the programme to continue. When it has finished, another beep will sound. Take out risen dough, for baked bread hold the tin handles. The bread can be removed at this stage by holding the tin handles with oven gloves and simply lifting it out of the machine. Alternatively, the bread may be left in the machine and will be kept hot for up to 90 minutes, depending on the length of the programme. Don't forget that the machine will be hot when you open the lid so try not to lean over the machine wearing glasses or contact lenses as they may steam up.

10 Removing the bread Holding the tin sides with oven gloves, loosen the bread from the tin with a plastic spatula or turn the tin upside down and shake several times. Once loosened, turn the bread out on to a wire rack and leave it to cool for at least 30 minutes to allow the steam to escape. The paddle or kneader blade should stay in the tin. If not, check the base of the bread and remove it carefully, remembering that it will be hot. Turn the machine off at the plug and leave it to cool.

Making bread by hand

WHAT TYPE OF YEAST CAN BE USED?
Recipes made in a bread machine have to be made with fast-action dried yeast. This can be used straight from the sachet. If you are making bread by hand, fresh yeast, dried yeast that requires frothing in water, as well as fast-action dried yeast can be used. The latter is by far the easiest and most convenient to use and is the one recommended for bread machine recipes.

1 Mixing Measure the flour into a large bowl then add the butter and rub it in with the fingertips until the mixture resembles fine breadcrumbs. Stir in the salt, milk powder, if using, sugar and fast-action dried yeast. Make a well in the centre of the flour then, using a wooden spoon, gradually mix in honey, maple syrup or malt extract, if using, and enough warm water to make a soft dough. When the dough begins to form, begin using your hands.

The amount of water given in the recipe is a guide and will vary depending on the type of flour used, the temperature in the kitchen and the level of humidity. Adjust the amount of water as needed and make the dough softer rather than firmer, if you are unsure.

2 Kneading This is essential to mix and activate the dried yeast and to help stretch the gluten in the flour so that the bread can rise fully. Begin by turning the dough out on to lightly floured surface. Stretch the dough by pushing the front half away with the heel of one hand while holding the back of the dough with the other hand. Fold the stretched part of the dough back on itself, give it a quarter turn and repeat for five more minutes, until the dough has been turned full circle several times and is a smooth and elastic ball.

3 First rising Dust the mixing bowl with a little extra flour, put the kneaded bread back

into the bowl and cover the top loosely with oiled clingfilm. Leave in a warm place to rise or 'prove' for about 1 hour or until the dough has doubled in size. This may take more or less time, depending on the temperature in the kitchen.

4 Knocking back Remove the clingfilm and save for the next rising. Knock back or punch the risen dough in the bowl with your fist to deflate it then pull it out of the bowl. Turn the dough out on to a lightly floured surface and knead well, as before.

5 Shaping Roll the dough back and forth with the palms of your hands in a rocking action until a rope of dough begins to form – about half as long again as the length of the loaf tin. Fold the end of the dough under so that it is an even width and the exact length of the tin then lay it in the greased tin. Cover loosely with oiled clingfilm.

6 Second rising and glazing Leave the bread in a warm place for 30 minutes for a second and final proving or until the dough rises just above the top of the tin. It is crucial not to over prove the dough at this stage or the bread may collapse in the oven. The dough is ready if when pressed lightly with a fingertip, the dent springs back slowly. If the dent stays as it is the bread is over proved. Remove the clingfilm and sprinkle with flour.

7 Baking and testing Bake bread in a preheated oven, 200°C (400°F), Gas Mark 6, for 25 minutes for a 500 g (1 lb) loaf, 30 minutes for a large 750 g (1½ lb) loaf or 35 minutes for an extra large 1 kg (2 lb) loaf. The bread should be well risen, golden brown and sound hollow when tapped with fingertips. Test the top then loosen the bread with a palette knife, holding the tin with oven gloves. Turn out on to a wire rack and tap the base of the bread to double check it is done. If the base feels a little soft, return it to the oven and place directly on to the oven shelf. Check again after 5 minutes and, if done transfer to wire rack to cool.

Tip Always leave hot bread to cool for at least 30 minutes before slicing.

Where is a warm place?
If your kitchen feels cold then try:
• Standing the bowl of dough over a large saucepan of just boiled water with the heat off, making sure that the water is not touching the base of the bowl.
• Standing the bowl of dough in a washing up bowl half filled with hot (but not boiling) water from the tap.
• Turning the main oven on to warm and placing the bowl of dough in the grill or oven above.
• If the central heating is on, standing the bowl of dough on a chair next to a radiator.

3

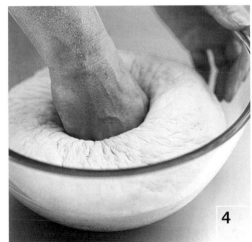

4

5

6a

6b

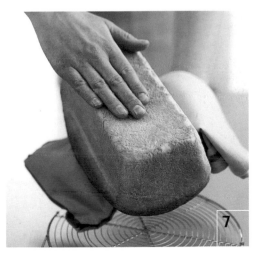

7

Shaping techniques

MAKING ENRICHED DOUGHS ▸

1 Roll the butter thinly between two sheets of nonstick or greaseproof paper then freeze it for 10 minutes. Knead and roll out the bread dough to a rectangle a little larger than butter.

2 Peel the paper off the butter and lay it over the dough.

3 Fold the bottom third of the dough up and over the butter.

4 Next, fold the top third of the dough up and over the bottom third. Give the dough a quarter turn and repeat the rolling and folding action, much like making flaky pastry. (For more detail, see page 108 for Croissants and page 109 for Danish Pastries.)

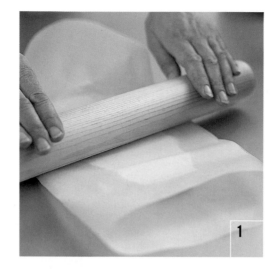

◂ COTTAGE LOAF OR LARGE BRIOCHE

1 Cut one-quarter off the dough. Shape the larger piece into a round ball and either put on to a greased baking sheet for a cottage loaf or into a large fluted tin for a brioche (see page 105 for individual brioche). Shape the smaller piece of dough into a ball then press on top of the larger one.

2 Secure the small ball of dough by pressing the floured handle of a wooden spoon down through the top of it and into the dough below. Use the same method for individual brioches using the handle of a teaspoon instead.

CROISSANTS ▸

1 Cut a large rectangle of dough into squares then halve each one to make triangles.

2 Roll each triangle up from the base towards the point then slightly curve the ends of the croissant towards each other (see page 108).

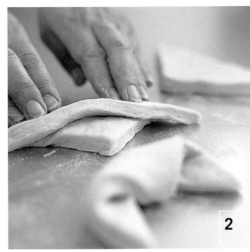

◂ PRETZELS

1 Curve a long thin rope of dough in a wide arc then, taking the ends of the rope in separate hands, twist the dough together about half way down the length.

2 Press the ends on to the sides of the loop to give the traditional knotted effect (see page 96).

◂ TWIST

Take a long thick rope of dough and holding one end firmly, twist the rope with the other hand to produce a corkscrew effect (see Carrot and Mustard Bread, page 64).

DOUBLE SLIT TWIST ▸

1 Roll out bread dough to a large square. Add flavourings, then roll up 'Swiss roll' style. Cut roll in half lengthways.

2 Carefully lift alternate strands over each other to give the twisted effect (see Feta and Spinach Twist, page 57).

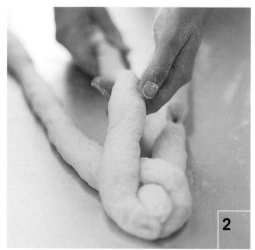

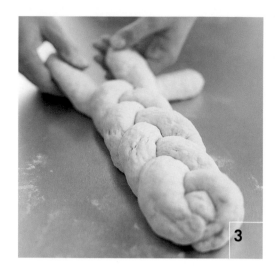

PLAIT ▲

1 Make three ropes of dough of the same length and equal thickness. Press them together at one end and arrange so that one runs straight downwards and the others are either side of it, at a slight angle. Bring the left-hand rope up and over the central rope so that this now forms the new central rope.

2 Bring the right-hand rope back over the new central rope and then repeat the process all over again, working from left to right and then back again.

3 For a straight plait continue until the ends of the bread ropes are reached then pinch them together so that they do not unravel.

4 To make a plaited ring, continue plaiting until almost at the end of the dough ropes, then curve the plait into a circle and tuck the ends together so that they go under and between the start of the plait neatly so it looks as if the plait runs continuously.

5 To make a traditional Jewish double plait, make a large plait as above and put on to a greased baking sheet. Make a second plait of the same length with thinner ropes of dough. Brush the top of the larger plait with beaten egg then press the thinner plait on top.

1

2

3

CUTTING DOUGH ▲

1 Make criss-cross lines over a floured loaf, before proving, using a sharp knife (see Buckwheat and Walnut Bread, page 47).

2 Slash the top of a just-risen loaf along it's length with a sharp knife or a new craft knife. It not only makes the bread look more interesting, but helps to speed up cooking.

3 Enlarge knife slits with a floured finger in flat breads such as Fougasse (see page 114).

◄ ADDING HOLES

For larger loaves, such as the Couronne (see page 50), make a small hole in the centre with a fingertip then gradually enlarge it by rolling the dough around a well floured fist.

For bagels (see page 104) and doughnuts (see page 100), insert a finger into the middle of a roll, then enlarge it with a second finger. Circle the bun around the fingers to enlarge further.

Finishing touches

COOKING BREADS ON THE HOB

1 Transfer risen bagels (see page 104) or pretzels (see page 96) with a flat slotted spoon into a large saucepan of just simmering water mixed with 1 tablespoon of caster sugar. Add just two or three breads at a time, depending on the size, and cook for 2–3 minutes until they float. Drain well then glaze and sprinkle with seeds for bagels or salt for pretzels, then bake for a wonderful unique chewy texture.

2 Transfer risen doughnuts (see page 100) to hot oil and fry until the underside is golden. Carefully turn them over with a slotted spoon and knife and cook the second side in the same way. Drain doughnuts well on kitchen paper, then sprinkle with cinnamon sugar.

3 Fry crumpets (see page 101) on a hot, lightly oiled frying or griddle pan until the base is browned and the top has bubbled and dried. Loosen and remove rings then turn the crumpets over and brown the tops.

4 Fry naan breads (see page 92) in a hot, lightly oiled frying or griddle pan until browned on both sides.

WHAT ABOUT BREADS BAKED IN A MACHINE?

Check with your machine manual and work out when the cooking will begin during the timed programme. Brush with your chosen glaze before cooking begins or up to 10 minutes into baking and sprinkle with seeds, flour or your chosen ingredient. Keep the lid of the bread machine open for the briefest time possible so that the heat does not drop too much.

Otherwise, leave the bread plain and glaze it after it is cooked. If the bread is a little pale at the end of cooking, brush with a glaze then brown under a hot grill.

GARNISHES AND DECORATIONS

Sprinkling the top of a shaped loaf or small roll can be a good way of indicating if the bread is sweet or savoury and helps to give a clue as to what is in the bread.

For savoury breads, try the following toppings: a little flour, barley flakes, porridge oats, cornmeal, wheat germ, linseeds, caraway, fennel, sunflower, sesame, pumpkin or poppy seeds, coarse salt flakes, paprika, dried chilli seeds, white or black mustard seeds, grated

Egg yolk and water: mix one egg yolk with 1 tablespoon cold water and brush over risen dough for a shiny glaze. Egg yolk mixed with water is much better than just a whole egg as this tends to go streaky during cooking.

Egg white and water: use 1 egg white mixed with 1 tablespoon cold water for a paler crust with a softer sheen.

Melted butter: can be brushed over breads before and after baking to darken the crust as it cooks and to help keep the baked crust soft.

Olive oil: can be drizzled over foccacia and other flat Mediterranean breads just as it goes into the oven and again for a soft glistening finish as it comes out. Choose virgin olive oil for a stronger, more intense flavour.

Salted water: mix 3 teaspoons salt with 3 table-spoons water and brush over risen dough just before baking for a crisp crust. To make a less salty glaze, add 1 teaspoon caster sugar, if liked.

Milk wash: brush this over white risen dough for a soft crust and as a 'glue' for sticking grains and seeds on to the top of breads

Milk and sugar glaze: dissolve 2 tablespoons caster sugar in 4 tablespoons milk then boil for 1 minute. Brush over just-baked sweet breads, malt breads and hot cross buns for an extremely glossy finish.

Preserves: warm 3 tablespoons marmalade or apricot jam with 1–2 tablespoons water, orange juice, brandy or liqueur for a sticky glaze to apply after baking to teabreads, gingerbread, Danish pastries, sweet rolls or other sweet breads.

Honey or golden syrup: warm a little in the microwave or a small pan and then brush over the top of a just-baked loaf or rolls for a very sticky but highly glossy glaze.

Glacé icing: mix 125 g (4 oz) sifted icing sugar with 4–5 teaspoons fresh lemon or orange juice or water to make a thin-coating icing and drizzle from a spoon or brush over hot or cold sweet loaves or rolls.

cheese, fresh herbs, sliced tomatoes. Be wary of using sun-dried tomatoes unless stored in oil as these scorch quickly during baking.

For a sweet topping, try: white or coloured sugars, icing sugar, roughly crushed sugar lumps, brown coffee crystals, strips of citron peel, roughly chopped nuts, dried fruits, grated or chopped chocolate or cocoa.

GLAZES AND FINISHES

Brushing a glaze over the shaped dough just before baking enhances the colour and sheen of the bread and adds extra flavour to the crust. It takes only a matter of minutes to do, but gives a professional-looking finish.

Baking know-how

KEEPING BREAD DOUGH

If you find you suddenly get interrupted and don't have time to shape and bake the bread dough as planned, then it can be stored for several hours or overnight in the fridge, tightly covered with oiled clingfilm. Knock the dough back once or twice if it gets very big. Allow the dough to come to room temperature then knead it well, shape and then leave for a final rising in a warm place until it is half as big again. Bake as the recipe.

Storing dough can be particularly useful when making croissants and Danish pastries as they can be left half way through the rolling and folding stage. Shaped breads can be stored in the fridge for several hours and then baked when ready, if preferred.

ADDING MOISTURE

Adding a burst of steam in the oven while the bread is baking helps to keep the top of the bread soft at the beginning of baking so that the bread can rise to it's fullest potential. Once the heat has set the bread, the water aids the formation of a crisp crust.

Water sprayer: quickly spray a thick mist of water as soon as the bread has gone into the oven. Repeat twice more at three minute intervals, making sure to spray only the walls of the cooker and not the light or fan and keeping the oven door open for the shortest possible time.

Bowl of iced water: for a slower, more steady release of moisture, put a roasting tin of cold water and ice below the bread during baking.

Baker's stone: for a crisp crust, warm a baker's stone on the lowest shelf of the oven for 30 minutes. Alternatively, improvise with four unglazed terracotta tiles, making sure there is a gap around the outer edges for the heat to circulate. Place the bread dough straight on to the hot tiles and leave to cook. The tiles will keep the heat constant and draw the moisture from the bread to produce a really crisp crust. Traditionally a peel or baker's shovel would have been used to transfer the bread to the oven but a couple of oiled fish slices can be used instead.

STORING BREAD

Homemade bread is best eaten fresh on the day it is made, but can be kept fresh for a day or two with the addition of butter or oil. Unlike shop-bought bread, there are no preservatives to increase storage life, but the delicious taste means that homemade bread generally gets eaten before it has a chance to go stale.

Tip Rather than buying lots of different tins for baking, a multi-way rectangular tin with moveable dividers can give lots of options for square or rectangular loaves. As it folds flat, it takes up only the minimum of cupboard space.

Which tin to choose?

Traditionally bread tins came in standard 1 lb and 2 lb tins. However, with the advent of metric measurements, they are now sold in a confusing mixture of litre (pint) capacity, linear measurements, as well as the old imperial measurements. There is also now a wider choice of tin shape too, including round, springform tins, extra long loaf tins and mini tins.

Any leftovers that you may have can be wrapped in foil or a plastic bag if the bread has a soft crust, or in a paper bag, fabric bag or bread bin if it is a crusty loaf. Use the following day in sandwiches or for breakfast toast. Do not keep bread in the fridge as the cold draws the moisture out of it, making it dry.

For a longer shelf life, wrap cooled bread in a plastic bag and freeze until required. Or cut the loaf in half and eat half and freeze half. Perhaps the most useful way to freeze bread is in rolls or slices as you can take what you need out of the freezer when you need it.

everyday breads

Quick white loaf

SMALL 500 G (1 LB):

325 g (11 oz, 3 cups) strong
   white flour

1 tablespoon milk powder

2 teaspoons caster sugar

½ teaspoon salt

1¾ teaspoons fast-action dried
   yeast

1 tablespoon sunflower oil

200 ml (7 fl oz, scant 1 cup)
   warm water

LARGE 750 G (1½ LB):

500 g (1 lb, 4½ cups) strong
   white flour

2 tablespoons milk powder

1 tablespoon caster sugar

1 teaspoon salt

2½ teaspoons fast-action dried
   yeast

2 tablespoons sunflower oil

300 ml (½ pint, 1¼ cups) warm
   water

EXTRA LARGE 1 KG (2 LB):

625 g (1¼ lb, 5⅔ cups) strong
   white flour

3 tablespoons milk powder

4 teaspoons caster sugar

1½ teaspoons salt

2¾ teaspoons fast-action dried
   yeast

3 tablespoons sunflower oil

400 ml (14 fl oz, 1¾ cups) warm
   water

To make by hand

1 Mix the flour, milk powder, sugar, salt and yeast in a
   large bowl. Add the oil and gradually mix in enough
   warm water to make a soft dough.

2 Knead well on a lightly floured surface for 10 minutes
   until the dough is smooth and elastic. Put into a
   greased 500 g (1 lb), 1 kg (2 lb) or 1.8 litre (3 pint)
   loaf tin, depending on the size of the dough.

3 Cover loosely with oiled clingfilm and leave in a warm
   place to rise for 45 minutes or until the dough
   reaches just above the top of the tin.

4 Remove the clingfilm and bake in a preheated oven,
   200°C (400°F), Gas Mark 6, for 25 minutes for the
   small loaf, 30 minutes for the large and 35 minutes
   for the extra large, or until the bread is golden brown
   and sounds hollow when tapped with the fingertips.
   Check larger loaves after 15 minutes and cover with
   foil if overbrowning.

5 Holding the tin with oven gloves, loosen the bread
   with a palette knife. Transfer to a wire rack to cool.

To make with a breadmaker

1 Lift the tin out of the bread machine, fit the kneader
   blade then add the measured water, milk powder
   and oil. Spoon in the flour then add the sugar and
   salt. Make a slight dip in the centre of the flour and
   sprinkle in the yeast (see page 14).

2 Insert the tin into the bread machine. Shut the lid
   and set to rapid/fastbake and select the size of loaf.
   (This programme does not usually give an option for
   crust colour.) Press start.

3 At the end of the programme, lift the tin out of the
   machine with oven gloves. Loosen the bread with a
   plastic spatula then turn out on to a wire rack and
   leave to cool.

Makes 1 loaf

Tips This is one of the few times that warm water
is needed in a bread machine. Ideally it should
be 30–35°C (85–90°F), warm enough to get the
yeast going as soon as it comes into contact with
the water.

   Bread made on a rapid cycle or fastbake
programme in a bread machine is best taken out
of the tin as soon as it is cooked as the moisture
present at the end of cooking will make the loaf
go soggy as it cools.

Rapid light wholemeal loaf

This loaf is a good halfway stage for children who are reluctant brown bread eaters as it is made, quite literally, with half wholemeal and half white flour.

SMALL 500 G (1 LB):

175 g (6 oz, 1½ cups) strong wholemeal flour

150 g (5 oz, 1⅓ cups) strong white flour

2 teaspoons caster sugar

½ teaspoon salt

1¾ teaspoons fast-action dried yeast

1 tablespoon sunflower oil

200 ml (7 fl oz, scant 1 cup) warm water

LARGE 750 G (1½ LB):

250 g (8 oz, 2¼ cups) strong wholemeal flour

250 g (8 oz, 2¼ cups) strong white flour

1 tablespoon caster sugar

1 teaspoon salt

2½ teaspoons fast-action dried yeast

2 tablespoons sunflower oil

300 ml (½ pint, 1¼ cups) warm water

EXTRA LARGE 1 KG (2 LB):

325 g (11 oz, 3 cups) strong wholemeal flour

300 g (10 oz, 2⅔ cups) strong white flour

4 teaspoons caster sugar

1½ teaspoons salt

2¾ teaspoons fast-action dried yeast

3 tablespoons sunflower oil

400 ml (14 fl oz, 1¾ cups) warm water

To make by hand

1 Mix the flours, sugar, salt and yeast in a large bowl. Add the oil and gradually mix in enough warm water to make a soft dough.

2 Knead well on a lightly floured surface for 10 minutes until the dough is smooth and elastic. Put into a greased 500 g (1 lb), 1 kg (2 lb) or 1.8 litre (3 pint) loaf tin, depending on the size of the dough.

3 Cover loosely with oiled clingfilm and leave in a warm place to rise for 45 minutes or until the dough reaches just above the top of the tin.

4 Remove the clingfilm and bake in a preheated oven, 200°C (400°F), Gas Mark 6, for 25 minutes for the small loaf, 30 minutes for the large and 35 minutes for the extra large, or until the bread is browned and sounds hollow when tapped with the fingertips. Check after 15 minutes and cover with foil if overbrowning.

5 Holding the tin with oven gloves, loosen the bread with a palette knife. Transfer to a wire rack to cool.

> **Tip** Check your bread machine cookbook to make sure you use the right amount of yeast and the correct loaf size for your machine.

To make with a breadmaker

1 Lift the tin out of the bread machine, fit the kneader blade then add the measured water and oil. Spoon the flours in, then add the sugar and salt. Make a slight dip in the centre of the flour and sprinkle in the yeast (see page 14).

2 Insert the tin into the bread machine. Shut the lid and set to rapid/fastbake and select the size of loaf. Press start.

3 At the end of the programme, lift the tin out of the machine with oven gloves. Loosen the bread with a plastic spatula then turn out on to a wire rack and leave to cool.

Makes 1 loaf

Farmhouse white loaf

An ideal everyday loaf that makes the most of your breadmaker – light, fluffy and easy to slice, perfect for packed lunches and toast, or simply spread with butter and jam.

SMALL 500 G (1 LB)

300 g (10 oz, 2⅔ cups) strong white flour

1 tablespoon butter

1 teaspoon sugar

½ teaspoon salt

1 teaspoon fast-action dried yeast

175 ml (6 fl oz, ¾ cup) warm water

LARGE 750 G (1½ LB)

475 g (15 oz, 4⅓ cups) strong white flour

2 tablespoons butter

1½ teaspoons sugar

1 teaspoon salt

1¼ teaspoons fast-action dried yeast

275 ml (9 fl oz, 1 cup plus 2 tablespoons) warm water

EXTRA LARGE 1 KG (2 LB)

625 g (1¼ lb, 5⅔ cups) strong white flour

3 tablespoons butter

2 teaspoons sugar

1½ teaspoons salt

1½ teaspoons fast-action dried yeast

400 ml (14 fl oz, 1¾ cups) warm water

To make by hand

1 Put the flour into a large bowl, add the butter and rub in with the fingertips until the mixture resembles fine breadcrumbs. Stir in the sugar, salt and yeast. Gradually mix in enough warm water to make a soft dough.

2 Knead well on a lightly floured surface for 5 minutes until the dough is smooth and elastic. Put the dough back into the bowl, cover loosely with oiled clingfilm and leave in a warm place to rise for 45 minutes or until doubled in size.

3 Tip the dough out on to a lightly floured surface, knead well then put into a greased 500 g (1 lb), 1 kg (2 lb) or 1.8 litre (3 pint) loaf tin, depending on the size of the dough.

4 Cover loosely with oiled clingfilm and leave in a warm place to rise for 30 minutes or until the dough reaches the top of the tin.

5 Remove the clingfilm, sprinkle with flour and bake in a preheated oven, 200°C (400°F), Gas Mark 6, for 25 minutes for the small loaf, 30 minutes for the large and 35 minutes for the extra large, covering with foil after 20 minutes to prevent overbrowning.

6 Holding the tin with oven gloves, loosen the bread with a palette knife. Transfer to a wire rack to cool.

To make with a breadmaker

1 Lift the tin out of the bread machine, fit the kneader blade then add the measured cold water and butter. Spoon in the flour then add the sugar and salt. Make a slight dip in the centre of the flour and sprinkle in the yeast (see page 14).

2 Insert the tin into the bread machine. Shut the lid and set to basic white bread/size of loaf/bake and medium crust. Press start.

3 At the end of the programme, lift the tin out of the machine with oven gloves. Loosen the bread with a plastic spatula then turn out on to a wire rack, dust with flour and leave to cool.

Makes 1 loaf

> **Tip** For a richer, golden crust add 2 teaspoons of milk powder for a small loaf, 1 tablespoon for a large one and 2 tablespoons for an extra large one.

White soft grain loaf

SMALL 500 G (1 LB):

15 g (½ oz, 1 tablespoon) mixed groats

300 g (10 oz, 2⅔ cups) strong white flour

½ teaspoon salt

1 teaspoon caster sugar

25 g (1 oz, 2 tablespoons) millet flakes

1 teaspoon fast-action dried yeast

1 tablespoon sunflower oil

150 ml (5 fl oz, ⅔ cup) water

LARGE 750 G (1½ LB):

25 g (1 oz, 2 tablespoons) mixed groats

400 g (13 oz, 3⅔ cups) strong white flour

1 teaspoon salt

2 teaspoons caster sugar

50 g (2 oz, ¼ cup) millet flakes

1¼ teaspoons fast-action dried yeast

2 tablespoons sunflower oil

250 ml (8 fl oz, 1 cup) water

EXTRA LARGE 1 KG (2 LB):

50 g (2 oz, ¼ cup) mixed groats

550 g (1 lb 2 oz, 5 cups) strong white flour

1½ teaspoons salt

3 teaspoons caster sugar

75 g (3 oz, ¼ cup plus 2 tablespoons) millet flakes

1½ teaspoons fast-action dried yeast

3 tablespoons sunflower oil

350 ml (12 fl oz, 1½ cups) water

To make by hand

1 Begin as step 1, right.

2 Put the flour, salt, sugar and millet flakes into a large bowl. Stir in the yeast then add the oil, all but 1 tablespoon of the drained cooked groats and enough warm water to mix to a soft dough.

3 Knead well on a lightly floured surface for 5 minutes until the dough is smooth and elastic. Put the dough back into the bowl, cover loosely with oiled clingfilm and leave in a warm place to rise for 1 hour or until doubled in size.

4 Tip the dough out on to a lightly floured surface, knead well then press into a greased 500 g (1 lb), 1 kg (2 lb) or 1.8 litre (3 pint) loaf tin, depending on the size of the dough.

5 Cover loosely with oiled clingfilm and leave in a warm place to rise for 30 minutes or until the dough reaches the top of the tin.

6 Remove the clingfilm, sprinkle with the remaining groats and bake in a preheated oven, 200°C (400°F), Gas Mark 6, for 25 minutes for the small loaf, 30 minutes for the large and 35 minutes for the extra large, or until the bread is golden and sounds hollow when tapped with the fingertips. Check the larger loaves after 15 minutes and cover with foil if overbrowning.

7 Holding the tin with oven gloves, loosen the bread with a palette knife. Transfer to a wire rack to cool.

To make with a breadmaker

1 Put the groats in a small saucepan, cover with cold water, bring to the boil then cook for 2 minutes. Drain and leave to cool.

2 Lift the tin out of the bread machine, fit the kneader blade then add the measured water, oil and all but 1 tablespoon of the drained cooked groats. Spoon in the millet flakes and flour then add the sugar and salt. Make a slight dip in the centre of the flour and sprinkle in the yeast (see page 14).

3 Insert the tin into the bread machine. Shut the lid and set to basic white bread/size of loaf/bake and medium crust. Press start. Sprinkle the reserved groats over the dough just before baking begins. Close the lid gently and leave the programme to continue.

4 At the end of the programme, lift the tin out of the machine with oven gloves. Loosen the bread with a plastic spatula then turn out on to a wire rack and leave to cool.

Makes 1 loaf

Tip Mixed groats are tiny cleaned and chopped grains, similar in size to pinhead oats, and provide extra protein in this recipe. They are available in health food shops.

Granary bread

SMALL 500 G (1 LB):

300 g (10 oz, 2⅔ cups) granary flour

1 tablespoon butter

1 teaspoon salt

2 teaspoons brown sugar

1 teaspoon fast-action dried yeast

200 ml (7 fl oz, scant 1 cup) water

LARGE 750 G (1½ LB):00 g

(1 lb, 4½ cups) granary flour

2 tablespoons butter

1½ teaspoons salt

1 tablespoon brown sugar

1¼ teaspoons fast-action dried yeast

300 ml (½ pint, 1¼ cups) water

EXTRA LARGE 1 KG (2 LB):

625 g (1¼ lb, 5⅝ cups) granary flour

3 tablespoons butter

2 teaspoons salt

4 teaspoons brown sugar

1½ teaspoons fast-action dried yeast

400 ml (14 fl oz, 1¾ cups) water

To make by hand

1 Put the flour into a large bowl, add the butter and rub in with the fingertips until the mixture resembles fine breadcrumbs. Stir in the salt, sugar and yeast then gradually mix in enough warm water to make a soft dough.

2 Knead on a lightly floured surface for 5 minutes until the dough is smooth and elastic. Put back into the bowl, cover loosely with oiled clingfilm and leave in a warm place to rise for 1 hour or until doubled in size.

3 Tip the dough out on to a lightly floured surface and knead well, adding flour to the surface to stop the dough sticking, if needed. Press into a greased 500 g (1 lb), 1 kg (2 lb) or 1.8 litre (3 pint) loaf tin, depending on the size of the dough.

4 Cover loosely with oiled clingfilm and leave for 30 minutes or until the dough reaches the top of the tin.

5 Remove the clingfilm and bake in a preheated oven, 200°C (400°F), Gas Mark 6, for 25–30 minutes for the small loaf, 30–35 minutes for the large and 35–40 minutes for the extra large, or until the bread is browned and sounds hollow when tapped with the fingertips. Check the larger loaves after 15 minutes and cover with foil if overbrowning.

6 Holding the tin with oven gloves, loosen the bread with a palette knife. Transfer to a wire rack to cool.

To make with a breadmaker

1 Lift the tin out of the bread machine, fit the kneader blade then add the measured cold water and butter. Spoon in the flour, then add the salt and sugar. Make a slight dip in the centre of the flour and sprinkle in the yeast (see page 14).

2 Insert the tin into the bread machine. Shut the lid and set to wholewheat/size of loaf/bake and select the preferred crust setting. Press start.

3 At the end of the programme, lift the tin out of the machine with oven gloves. Loosen the bread with a plastic spatula then turn out on to a wire rack and leave to cool.

Makes 1 loaf

> **Tip** Granary loaves can be heavy, so either add a little extra yeast to larger loaves, or a little lemon juice or crushed vitamin C tablets. (See your bread machine cookbook for more specific information.)

Wheat germ and honey bread

During milling, wheat germ is removed from white flour. It has been re-introduced in this tasty sandwich loaf for added nutritional value.

475 g (15 oz, 4⅓ cups) strong white flour

50 g (2 oz, ¼ cup) wheat germ

1 teaspoon salt

2 tablespoons butter

1¼ teaspoons fast-action dried yeast

2 teaspoons clear honey

275 ml (9 fl oz, 1 cup plus 2 tablespoons) water

1 egg yolk, to glaze

2 tablespoons sesame seeds

To make by hand

1 Put the flour, wheat germ and salt into a large bowl. Add the butter and rub in with the fingertips until the mixture resembles fine breadcrumbs. Stir in the yeast, then add the honey and gradually mix in enough warm water to make a soft dough.

2 Knead well on a lightly floured surface for 5 minutes until the dough is smooth and elastic. Put the dough back into the bowl, cover loosely with oiled clingfilm and leave in a warm place to rise for 1 hour or until doubled in size.

3 Tip the dough out on to a lightly floured surface and knead well. Shape into a large oval about 23 cm (9 inches) long then transfer to a greased baking sheet and make slashes along the top at 2.5 cm (1 inch) intervals with a sharp knife.

4 Cover loosely with oiled clingfilm and leave to rise for 30 minutes or until half as big again.

5 Brush with the egg yolk mixed with 1 tablespoon of water and bake in a preheated oven, 200°C (400°F), Gas Mark 6, for 10 minutes. Brush with egg again then sprinkle with the sesame seeds. Bake for 15–20 minutes more until the bread is deep golden brown and sounds hollow when tapped with the fingertips. Check after 10 minutes and cover with foil if overbrowning.

6 Holding the tin with oven gloves, loosen the bread with a palette knife. Transfer to a wire rack to cool.

To make with a breadmaker

1 Lift the tin out of the bread machine, fit the kneader blade then add the measured cold water, butter and honey. Spoon the flour and wheat germ over the top then add the salt. Make a slight dip in the centre of the flour and sprinkle in the yeast (see page 14).

2 Insert the tin into the bread machine. Shut the lid and set to dough or basic dough. Press start.

3 At the end of the programme, lift the tin out of the machine and tip the dough out on to a lightly floured surface. Continue as step 3, left.

Makes 1 large loaf

Oat and molasses bread

475 g (15 oz, 4⅓ cups) strong
   wholemeal flour

2 tablespoons butter

¼ plain or orange flavoured
   1000 mg vitamin C tablet

1½ teaspoons salt

4 teaspoons molasses sugar

100 g (3½ oz, ½ cup) rolled oats

1¼ teaspoons fast-action dried
   yeast

350 ml (12 fl oz, 1½ cups) water

To make by hand

1 Put the flour into a large bowl, add the butter and rub in with fingertips until the mixture resembles fine breadcrumbs. Crush the vitamin C tablet between 2 teaspoons then stir into the flour along with the salt, sugar, oats and yeast. Gradually mix in enough warm water to make a soft dough.

2 Knead well on a lightly floured surface for 5 minutes until the dough is smooth and elastic. Put the dough back into the bowl, cover loosely with oiled clingfilm and leave in a warm place to rise for 1 hour or until doubled in size.

3 Tip the dough out on to a lightly floured surface and knead well. Press into a greased 20 cm (8 inch) deep round cake tin.

4 Cover loosely with oiled clingfilm and leave in a warm place to rise for 30 minutes or until the dough just reaches the top of the tin.

5 Remove the clingfilm and bake in a preheated oven, 200°C (400°F), Gas Mark 6, for 35–40 minutes until the bread is deep brown and sounds hollow when tapped with the fingertips.

6 Holding the tin with oven gloves, loosen the bread with a palette knife. Transfer to a wire rack to cool.

To make with a breadmaker

1 Lift the tin out of the bread machine, fit the kneader blade then add the measured cold water, butter and sugar. Spoon in the flour, oats and salt. Make a slight dip in the centre of the flour, crush the piece of vitamin C tablet between 2 teaspoons then add to the tin with the yeast (see page 14).

2 Insert the tin into the bread machine. Shut the lid and set to wholewheat/large 750 g (1½ lb) loaf/bake and select the preferred crust setting. Press start.

3 At the end of the programme, lift the tin out of the machine with oven gloves. Loosen the bread with a plastic spatula then turn out on to a wire rack and leave to cool.

Makes 1 large loaf

Tip If you don't have any molasses sugar then treacle can be used instead.

Golden linseed and spelt bread

Stoneground from an ancient wheat variety first grown by the Romans, spelt flour is unbleached with a fuller flavour that goes particularly well with the nuttiness of the golden linseeds.

475 g (15 oz, 4⅓ cups) spelt flour

1 teaspoon salt

1 tablespoon soft light brown sugar

50 g (2 oz, ¼ cup) golden linseeds

2½ teaspoons fast-action dried yeast

2 tablespoons sunflower oil

300 ml (½ pint, 1¼ cups) warm water

milk, to glaze

extra golden linseeds

To make by hand

1 Put the flour into a large bowl and mix in the salt, sugar, linseeds and yeast. Add the oil then gradually mix in enough warm water to make a soft dough.

2 Knead well on a lightly floured surface for 5 minutes until the dough is smooth and elastic. Shape into an oval loaf about 23 cm (9 inches) long, put on to a greased baking sheet and slash along its length with a knife.

3 Cover loosely with oiled clingfilm and leave in a warm place to rise for 45 minutes until half as big again.

4 Remove the clingfilm, brush the bread with milk and sprinkle with extra linseeds. Bake in a preheated oven, 200°C (400°F), Gas Mark 6, for 25–30 minutes until the bread is well risen, browned and sounds hollow when tapped with the fingertips.

5 Holding the sheet with oven gloves, loosen the bread with a palette knife. Transfer to a wire rack to cool.

To make in a breadmaker

1 Lift the tin out of the bread machine, fit the kneader blade then add the measured warm water and oil. Spoon in the flour, salt, sugar and linseeds. Make a slight dip in the centre of the flour and sprinkle in the yeast (see page 14).

2 Insert the tin into the bread machine. Brush with milk and extra linseeds, if liked. Shut the lid and set to rapid/fastbake/large 750 g (1½ lb) loaf and select the preferred crust setting. Press start.

3 At the end of the programme, lift the tin out of the machine with oven gloves. Loosen the bread with a plastic spatula then turn out on to a wire rack and leave to cool.

Makes 1 large loaf

> **Tip** If making bread with spelt flour on one of the longer settings on a bread machine, then use half spelt flour and half strong white flour or the loaf may have a rather close and dense finished texture.

2 rustic breads

Mixed seed bread

Made with malthouse flour, a blend of white and rye flours mixed with wheat flakes and three different seeds, this bread has a deliciously nutty taste and is a good way of boosting vital minerals.

475 g (15 oz, 4⅓ cups)
   malthouse flour
2 tablespoons butter
1 tablespoon brown sugar
1½ teaspoons salt
3 tablespoons sesame seeds
3 tablespoons sunflower seeds
3 tablespoons linseeds
1¼ teaspoons fast-action dried
   yeast
300 ml (½ pint, 1¼ cups) water
milk to glaze
extra seeds, optional

To make by hand

1 Put the flour into a large bowl, add the butter and rub in with the fingertips until the mixture resembles fine breadcrumbs. Stir in the sugar, salt, seeds and yeast. Gradually mix in enough warm water to make a soft dough.

2 Knead well on a lightly floured surface for 5 minutes until the dough is smooth and elastic. Put back into the bowl, cover loosely with oiled clingfilm and leave in a warm place to rise for 1 hour or until doubled in size.

3 Turn out on to a lightly floured surface and knead again for 5 minutes. Put the dough into a greased 20 cm (8 inch) round loose-bottomed tin.

4 Cover loosely with oiled clingfilm and leave in a warm place to rise for 30 minutes or until the dough reaches the top of the tin.

5 Remove the clingfilm, brush the top with a little milk and sprinkle with some extra seeds. Bake in a preheated oven, 200°C (400°F), Gas Mark 6, for 30–35 minutes or until the bread is well risen, golden and sounds hollow when tapped. Cover with foil after 15 minutes to prevent overbrowning.

6 Holding the tin with oven gloves, loosen the bread with a palette knife. Transfer to a wire rack to cool.

To make with a breadmaker

1 Lift the tin out of the bread machine, fit the kneader blade then add the measured cold water and butter. Spoon in the flour then add the sugar, salt and seeds. Make a slight dip in the centre of the flour and sprinkle in the yeast (see page 14).

2 Insert the tin into the bread machine. Shut the lid and set to wholewheat/large 750 g (1½ lb) loaf/bake and select the preferred crust setting. Press start.

3 Just before baking begins, brush the top of the dough with a little milk and sprinkle over some extra seeds, if liked, shut the lid and continue the programme.

4 At the end of the programme, lift the tin out of the machine with oven gloves. Loosen the bread with a plastic spatula then turn out on to a wire rack and leave to cool.

Makes 1 large loaf

Sage and Parmesan flutes

These thin baguette-style breads are delicious served with tomato-tossed pasta dishes or used as the base for bruschetta-style hot open sandwiches. Use leftovers to make tasty croutons to sprinkle on soup.

500 g (1 lb, 4½ cups) malthouse
flour

65 g (2½ oz, ¼ cup) Parmesan
cheese, grated

3 tablespoons fresh chopped sage
or 2 teaspoons dried

1½ teaspoons salt

1½ teaspoons fast-action dried
yeast

3 tablespoons olive oil

1 tablespoon honey

300 ml (½ pint, 1¼ cups) water

extra flour or Parmesan for
dusting

To make by hand

1 Put the flour into a large bowl. Stir in the cheese, sage, salt and yeast. Add the oil and honey, then gradually mix in enough warm water to make a smooth soft dough.

2 Knead well on a floured surface for 5 minutes until the dough is smooth and elastic. Put it back into the bowl, cover loosely with oiled clingfilm and leave the dough to rise in a warm place for 1 hour or until doubled in size.

3 Tip the dough out on to a floured surface, knead well then cut into 3 equal-sized pieces. Roll each piece into a 30 cm (12 inch) length and then transfer it to a large greased baking sheet. Leaving enough space between the loaves to allow them to rise.

4 Make diagonal cuts along the top of each loaf, at intervals. Cover loosely with oiled clingfilm and leave in a warm place for 30 minutes until well risen.

5 Sprinkle the loaves with a little extra flour or Parmesan and bake in a preheated oven, 200°C (400°F), Gas Mark 6, for 15 minutes until well risen and golden and the bread sounds hollow when tapped with the fingertips.

6 Holding the tin with oven gloves, loosen the bread with a palette knife. Transfer to a wire rack to cool.

To make with a breadmaker

1 Lift the tin out of the bread machine, fit the kneader blade then add the measured cold water, oil, honey, Parmesan and sage. Spoon in the flour, then add the salt. Make a slight dip in the centre and sprinkle in the yeast (see page 14).

2 Insert the tin into the bread machine. Shut the lid and set to dough or basic dough only. Press start.

3 At the end of the programme, lift the tin out of the bread machine, tip the dough on to a floured work surface and continue as step 3, left.

Makes 3 loaves

Tip In place of sage, try fresh basil, marjoram or chopped chives, or dried herbes de Provence.

Fruited muesli bread

475 g (15 oz, 4⅓ cups) strong
   white flour
2 tablespoons milk powder
3 tablespoons soft light brown
   sugar
1 teaspoon salt
1 teaspoon ground cinnamon
2 tablespoons butter
100 g (3½ oz, ½ cup) fruit muesli
1¼ teaspoons fast-action dried
   yeast
300 ml (½ pint, 1¼ cups) water
100 g (3½ oz, ½ cup) ready-to-eat
   dried apricots
50 g (2 oz, ¼ cup) dried
   cranberries

TO FINISH:
1 egg yolk, to glaze
3 tablespoons muesli, to decorate

To make by hand

1 Put the flour, milk powder, sugar, salt and cinnamon into a large bowl. Add the butter and rub in with the fingertips until the mixture resembles fine breadcrumbs. Stir in the muesli and yeast then gradually mix in enough warm water to mix to a soft dough.

2 Knead on a lightly floured surface for 5 minutes until smooth and elastic then put back into the bowl, cover with oiled clingfilm and leave to rise in a warm place for 1 hour or until doubled in size.

3 Tip the dough out on to the work surface, knead well then gradually work in the chopped apricots and cranberries.

4 Shape the dough into a round then press into a greased 20 cm (8 inch) springform tin. Cover loosely with oiled clingfilm and leave to rise for 30 minutes or until the dough is at the top of the tin.

5 Remove the clingfilm, brush the top of the bread with the egg yolk mixed with 1 tablespoon water. Sprinkle with extra muesli and bake in a preheated oven, 200°C (400°F), Gas Mark 6, for 35–40 minutes until well risen and the bread sounds hollow when tapped with the fingertips. Cover with foil after 15 minutes to prevent overbrowning.

6 Holding the tin with oven gloves, loosen the bread with a palette knife. Transfer to a wire rack to cool.

To make with a breadmaker

1 Take the loaf tin out of the bread machine, fit the kneader blade then add the measured cold water, milk powder, butter, sugar, salt and cinnamon.

2 Spoon the flour and muesli over the top then make a slight dip and sprinkle in the yeast (see page 14).

3 Insert the tin into the bread machine. Shut the lid and set to dough or basic dough. Press start.

4 At the end of the programme, lift the tin out of the machine, tip the dough out on to a floured work surface and continue as step 3, left.

Makes 1 extra large loaf

> **Tip** This bread can be mixed and baked in a bread machine fitted with a 2.5 litre (4 pint) bread tin, but halve the amount of fruit and add it at the raisin beep instead.

Lager-baked batons

Unusually, this bread is made with lager. But although these light and thin white batons rise beautifully, they have only the mildest hint of beer once baked. Serve with main meal salads or country-style meat pâtés.

425 g (14 oz, 3¾ cups plus 2
  tablespoons) strong white flour
1 teaspoon salt
1 teaspoon fast-action dried yeast
2 tablespoons olive oil
2 teaspoons clear honey
250 ml (8 fl oz, 1 cup) lager
extra flour for dusting

To make by hand

1 Put the flour, salt and yeast into a large bowl. Add the oil and honey. Gently warm the lager in a saucepan, then gradually add to the mixture to make a smooth soft dough.

2 Knead on a lightly floured surface for 10 minutes until smooth and elastic then put back into the bowl, cover with oiled clingfilm and leave to rise in a warm place for 1 hour or until doubled in size.

3 Tip the dough out on to a lightly-floured surface and knead well. Cut into 4 pieces and then roll each piece into a 30 cm (12 inches) length.

4 Transfer the dough to a large greased baking sheet, cover loosely with oiled clingfilm and leave for 30 minutes or until the dough is half as big again.

5 Dust with a little extra flour and bake in a preheated oven, 220°C, 425°F, Gas Mark 7, for 8–10 minutes until golden and the bread sounds hollow when tapped.

6 Holding the tin with oven gloves, loosen the bread with a palette knife. Transfer to a wire rack to cool.

To make with a breadmaker

1 Take the tin out of the bread machine, fit the kneader blade then add the lager, oil and honey. Spoon the flour over the top then add the salt, make a slight dip and sprinkle in the yeast (see page 14).

2 Insert the tin into the bread machine. Shut the lid and set to dough or basic dough. Press start.

3 At the end of the programme, lift the tin out of the machine, tip the dough out on to a floured work surface and continue as step 3, left.

Makes 4 loaves

Tip As this bread contains lager, do not use the delay timer facility.

Light rye and soured cream bread

This New England-style rye bread is much lighter than the more traditional Eastern European rye breads. Adding thick soured cream or crème fraîche adds a wonderful fluffiness to this bread and it makes a perfect smoked salmon sandwich.

175 g (6 oz, 1½ cups) rye flour

175 g (6 oz, 1½ cups) granary flour

125 g (4 oz, 1⅛ cups) strong white flour

2 teaspoons caraway seeds

1½ teaspoons salt

1¼ teaspoons fast-action dried yeast

150 ml (¼ pint, ⅔ cup) soured cream or crème fraîche

1 tablespoon fresh lemon juice

2 tablespoons molasses sugar

250 ml (8 fl oz, 1 cup) water

To make by hand

1 Put the flours into a large bowl. Stir in the caraway seeds, salt and yeast then add the soured cream, lemon juice and molasses sugar. Gradually add enough warm water to make a smooth soft dough.

2 Knead on a lightly floured surface for 5 minutes until the dough is smooth and elastic then put it back into the bowl. Cover loosely with oiled clingfilm and leave to rise in a warm place for 1 hour or until the dough has doubled in size.

3 Tip the dough out on to the work surface, knead well then shape into a round loaf about 15 cm (6 inches) in diameter.

4 Transfer to a greased baking sheet and make cuts across the top of the bread with a small sharp knife, like the spokes of a wheel. Cover with oiled clingfilm and leave to rise for 30 minutes until the dough is half as big again.

5 Remove the clingfilm and bake in a preheated oven, 200°C (400°F), Gas Mark 6, for 25–30 minutes until browned and the bread sounds hollow when tapped with the fingertips.

6 Holding the tin with oven gloves, loosen the bread with a palette knife. Transfer to a wire rack to cool.

To make with a breadmaker

1 Take the loaf tin out of the bread machine, fit the kneader blade then add the measured cold water, soured cream, lemon juice, molasses sugar and caraway seeds.

2 Spoon the flours over the top then add the salt. Make a slight dip and sprinkle in the yeast (see page 14).

3 Insert the tin into the bread machine. Shut the lid and set to dough only or basic dough. Press start.

4 At the end of the programme, lift the tin out of the machine, tip the dough out on to a floured work surface and continue as step 3, left.

Makes 1 large loaf

Buckwheat and walnut bread

175 g (6 oz, 1⅛ cups) buckwheat
   flour
150 g (5 oz, 1⅓ cups) strong
   wholemeal flour
150 g (5 oz, 1⅓ cups) strong
   white flour
1 tablespoons soft brown sugar
1½ teaspoons salt
1½ teaspoons fast-action dried
   yeast
2 tablespoons olive oil
325 ml (11 fl oz, 1⅜ cups) water
150 g (5 oz, heaping ½ cup)
   walnut pieces
extra flour for dusting

To make by hand

1 Mix the flours, sugar, salt and yeast in a large mixing
   bowl. Add the oil and mix in enough warm water to
   make a soft dough.

2 Knead well on a lightly floured surface for 5 minutes
   until the dough is smooth and elastic. Gradually work
   in the walnuts then put the dough back into the
   bowl. Cover loosely with oiled clingfilm and leave in a
   warm place to rise for 1 hour or until doubled in size.

3 Tip the dough out on to a lightly floured surface,
   knead well then shape it into an oval loaf about
   28 x 10 cm (11 x 4 inches).

4 Transfer to a greased baking sheet. Make criss-cross
   cuts over the top with a sharp knife (see page 21)
   then cover it loosely with oiled clingfilm and leave it
   to rise in a warm place for 30 minutes until it is half
   as big again.

5 Remove the clingfilm, sprinkle with a little flour and
   bake in a preheated oven, 200°C (400°F), Gas Mark
   6, for 20–25 minutes until browned and the bread
   sounds hollow when tapped with the fingertips.

6 Holding the tin with oven gloves, loosen the bread
   with a palette knife. Transfer to a wire rack to cool.

To make with a breadmaker

1 Lift the tin out of the bread machine, fit the kneader
   blade then add the measured cold water and oil.
   Spoon over the flours, add the sugar and salt then
   make a slight dip and sprinkle in the yeast (see
   page 14).

2 Insert the tin into the bread machine, shut the lid
   and set to dough or basic dough. Press start.

3 When the raisin beep sounds, add the walnuts then
   continue with the programme.

4 At the end of the programme, lift the tin out of the
   machine, tip the bread out on to a lightly floured
   work surface and continue as step 3, left.

Makes 1 large loaf

Black bread

Flavoured with rye flour, caraway seeds and barley wine, this distinctive Russian bread is quite unlike the more European-style breads. Serve cut into thin slices and topped with pickled cucumber and herrings or smoked salmon and cream cheese.

200 g (7 oz, 1¾ cups) rye flour

150 g (5 oz, 1⅓ cups) strong white flour

150 g (5 oz, 1⅓ cups) strong wholemeal flour

2 tablespoons powdered milk

1 tablespoon cocoa powder

1 teaspoon instant coffee granules

1 teaspoon salt

1 teaspoon caraway seeds

1¾ teaspoons fast-action dried yeast

2 tablespoons sunflower oil

3 tablespoons molasses sugar

275 ml (9 fl oz, 1 cup plus 2 tablespoons) can of barley wine

To make by hand

1 Put the flours, milk powder, cocoa, coffee, salt, caraway seeds and yeast into a large bowl. Add the oil and the molasses sugar. Gently warm the barley wine in a saucepan then gradually mix in enough barley wine to make a smooth soft dough.

2 Knead on a lightly floured surface for 10 minutes until the dough is smooth and elastic then put it back into the bowl, cover with oiled clingfilm and leave to rise in a warm place for 1¼ hours or until the dough has doubled in size.

3 Tip the dough out on to the work surface and knead well. Shape into a ball about 15 cm (6 inches) in diameter then transfer to a greased baking sheet. Make criss-cross cuts over the top with a small sharp knife then cover with oiled clingfilm and leave for 20–25 minutes until the dough is half as big again.

4 Bake in a preheated oven, 200°C (400°F), Gas Mark 6, for 25–30 minutes until the bread is dark brown and sounds hollow when tapped with the fingertips. Cover with foil after 15 minutes if overbrowning.

5 Holding the tin with oven gloves, loosen the bread with a palette knife. Transfer to a wire rack to cool.

To make with a breadmaker

1 Take the tin out of the bread machine, fit the kneader blade then add the barley wine, milk powder, oil, molasses sugar, cocoa, coffee and caraway seeds.

2 Spoon in the flours then add the salt, make a slight dip and sprinkle in the yeast (see page 14).

3 Insert the tin into the bread machine. Shut the lid and set to wholewheat/large 750 g (1½ lb) loaf/bake and select the preferred crust setting. Press start. Do not use the time delay option.

4 At the end of the programme, lift the tin out of the machine with oven gloves. Loosen the bread with a plastic spatula then turn out on to a wire rack and leave to cool.

Makes 1 large loaf

> **Tips** The bread can also be made to dough stage in a bread machine and then shaped by hand and baked in the oven.
>
> Brown ale or stout can also be used in place of the barley wine.

Ciabatta bread

Peppered with holes, this light airy Italian bread makes the perfect accompaniment to any meal. Unlike other breads, it is not kneaded, but left to rise and then simply spooned and pulled into shape so that the bubbles made by the yeast are kept intact.

FOR THE STARTER OR BIGA:

125 g (4 oz, 1⅛ cups) organic unbleached strong white flour

½ teaspoon caster sugar

½ teaspoon fast-action dried yeast

150 ml (¼ pint, ⅔ cup) warm water

FOR THE SECOND STAGE:

1 tablespoon milk powder

2 tablespoons olive oil

375 g (12 oz, 3½ cups) organic unbleached strong white flour

1 teaspoon salt

1 teaspoon caster sugar

1 teaspoon fast-action dried yeast

250 ml (8 fl oz, 1 cup) water

To make by hand

1 To make the starter, put the flour, sugar and yeast into a bowl and gradually mix in the warm water to make a smooth batter. Cover the bowl with a clean tea towel and leave overnight in a warm place.

2 For the second stage, add the milk powder, oil, flour, salt, sugar and yeast to the starter then gradually mix in the measured warm water to make a smooth, thick spoonable batter. Cover and leave in a warm place for 2 hours until the batter has tripled in size.

3 Grease a large baking sheet then sprinkle it with a little cornmeal or flour. Scrape the dough into 2 mounds on the baking sheet. With well-floured hands, gently pull the dough into 2 long loaves about 25 cm (10 inches) in length.

4 Leave in a warm place, uncovered, for 45 minutes or until half as big again. Bake in a preheated oven, 220°C, 425°F, Gas Mark 7, for 20–25 minutes until golden brown and the loaves sound hollow when tapped with the fingertips.

5 Holding the tin with oven gloves, loosen the bread with a palette knife. Transfer to a wire rack to cool.

Tip Keep an eye on the bread dough during its second time in the bread machine. If your bread tin is small, you may need to take it out of the machine 10–15 minutes before the end of the programme if the dough looks as if it may spill over the top.

To make with a breadmaker

1 First, to make the starter, lift the tin out of the bread machine, fit the kneader blade then add the measured cold water and spoon over the flour and sugar. Make a slight dip and sprinkle in the yeast (see page 14).

2 Insert the tin into the bread machine. Shut the lid and set to dough or basic dough. The dough will be very soft at this stage and look more like a batter than a bread dough. Turn off after 1 hour or before the mixture is kneaded for a second time. Leave to stand in the bread machine overnight.

3 For the second stage, take the tin out of the bread machine and add the milk powder, oil and measured cold water to the starter. Spoon in the flour, salt and sugar then sprinkle over the yeast.

4 Insert the tin back into the bread machine and set to dough again and leave to complete the programme.

5 The dough will be very sticky and soft at this stage. Continue as step 3, left.

Makes 2 loaves

Couronne

This loaf was originally shaped into a ring so that the French housewife could simply slip it over her arm when shopping. Traditionally, this loaf is made with a yeast starter that is left for two days, but this cheat's version is made with natural yogurt instead to give it the characteristic sourdough flavour.

500 g (1 lb, 4½ cups) unbleached strong white flour

1½ teaspoons salt

2 teaspoons caster sugar

1¼ teaspoons fast-action dried yeast

200 g (7 oz, ¾ cup plus 2 tablespoons) natural yogurt

175 ml (6 fl oz, ¾ cup) water

To make by hand

1 Put the flour into a large bowl then stir in the salt, sugar and yeast. Add the yogurt then gradually mix in enough warm water to make a soft dough.

2 Knead on a lightly floured surface for 5 minutes or until the dough is smooth and elastic. Put it back into the bowl, cover loosely with oiled clingfilm and leave to rise in a warm place for 1 hour or until it has doubled in size.

3 Tip the dough out on to a lightly-floured surface and knead well. Shape into a round then make a small hole in the centre with the fingertips, enlarge with a fist (see page 21) until the hole is about 12 cm (5 inches) wide and bread a ring of about 20 cm (8 inches) in diameter.

4 Transfer to a greased baking sheet and mark with 3 or 4 cuts if liked. Grease the base of a small basin and put it into the centre of the bread to keep the 'hole' intact. Cover the bread and basin loosely with oiled clingfilm and leave it in a warm place for 30 minutes or until it is half as big again.

5 Remove the clingfilm and basin, sprinkle the dough with flour and bake in a preheated oven, 220°C (420°F), Gas Mark 7, for 20–25 minutes until it is well risen and browned and the bread sounds hollow when tapped with the fingertips. Cover with foil after 15 minutes if overbrowning.

6 Holding the tin with oven gloves, loosen the bread with a palette knife. Transfer to a wire rack to cool.

To make with a breadmaker

1 Lift the tin out of the bread machine, fit the kneader blade then add the measured cold water and yogurt. Spoon in the flour, then add the salt and sugar. Make a slight dip and sprinkle in the yeast (see page 14).

2 Insert the tin into the bread machine. Shut the lid and set to dough only. Press start.

3 At the end of the programme, lift out the tin and tip the dough on to a lightly-floured surface. Continue as step 3, left.

Makes 1 loaf

Tip As this bread contains yogurt, do not use the delay timer facility.

Granary and pumpkin bread

475 g (15 oz, 4⅛ cups) granary
   flour

2 tablespoons butter

1½ teaspoons salt

50 g (2 oz, ¼ cup) pumpkin seeds

1¼ teaspoons fast-action dried
   yeast

¼ plain or orange flavoured 1000
   mg Vitamin C tablet

2 tablespoons malt extract

300 ml (½ pint, 1¼ cups) water

TO FINISH:

milk, to glaze

pumpkin seeds

To make by hand

1 Put the flour into a large bowl, add the butter and rub in with the fingertips until the mixture resembles fine breadcrumbs. Stir in the salt, pumpkin seeds and yeast. Crush the vitamin C tablet between 2 teaspoons and add to the bowl with the malt extract. Gradually mix in enough warm water to make a soft dough.

2 Tip the dough on to a lightly-floured work surface and knead for 5 minutes until it is smooth and elastic. Put it back into the bowl, cover loosely with oiled clingfilm and leave in a warm place for 1 hour or until it has doubled in size.

3 Tip the dough out on to a floured work surface, knead well then roll out and press into the base of a greased 1 kg (2 lb) loaf tin. Cover loosely with oiled clingfilm and leave to rise for 30 minutes or until the dough is just above the top of the tin.

4 Remove the clingfilm, brush the dough with milk and sprinkle with extra pumpkin seeds. Bake in a preheated oven, 200°C (400°F), Gas Mark 6, for 25–30 minutes, covering with foil after 15 minutes to prevent overbrowning.

5 Holding the tin with oven gloves, loosen the bread with a palette knife. Transfer to a wire rack to cool.

To make with a breadmaker

1 Remove the tin from the bread machine, fit the kneader blade then add the measured cold water, butter and malt extract. Spoon the flour over then add the salt and pumpkin seeds. Crush the piece of vitamin C tablet between 2 teaspoons and add to the flour. Make a slight dip in the centre of the flour and add the yeast (see page 14).

2 Insert the tin into the machine, close the lid and set to wholewheat/large 750 g (1½ lb) loaf bake and select the preferred crust setting. Press start.

3 Just before baking begins, brush the top of the bread with the milk and sprinkle over a few pumpkin seeds. Quickly shut the lid and continue the programme.

4 At the end of the programme, lift the tin out of the machine with oven gloves. Loosen the bread with a plastic spatula then turn out on to a wire rack and leave to cool.

Makes 1 large loaf

flavoured breads

Courgette, tarragon and lemon bread

An aromatic, tangy lemon bread speckled with just a hint of green. The ideal partner in a tuna fish sandwich or served with fish pâtés, dips or salads. Although the courgette has a very mild flavour it makes the bread deliciously light.

150 g (5 oz, heaping ½ cup) courgette

500 g (1 lb, 4½ cups) strong white flour

1 lemon, grated rind only

1 tablespoon fresh chopped tarragon

1 teaspoon caster sugar

2 teaspoons salt

freshly ground black pepper

1½ teaspoons fast-action dried yeast

2 tablespoons olive oil

200 ml (7 fl oz, scant 1 cup) water

To make by hand

1 Coarsely grate the courgette and pat dry with kitchen paper.

2 Put the flour into a large bowl then stir in the lemon rind, tarragon, sugar, salt, pepper and yeast. Add the courgette and oil then mix in enough warm water to make a soft dough.

3 Knead well on a lightly floured surface for 5 minutes until the dough is smooth and elastic. Put the dough back into the bowl, cover loosely with oiled clingfilm and leave in a warm place to rise for 1 hour or until doubled in size.

4 Tip the dough out on to a lightly floured surface, knead well and put into a greased 1 kg (2 lb) loaf tin.

5 Cover loosely with oiled clingfilm and leave in a warm place to rise for 30 minutes or until the dough reaches the top of the tin.

6 Remove the clingfilm and bake in a preheated oven, 200°C (400°F), Gas Mark 6, for 30 minutes until the bread is golden brown and sounds hollow when tapped with the fingertips. Check after 20 minutes and cover with foil if overbrowning.

7 Holding the tin with oven gloves, loosen the bread with a palette knife. Transfer to a wire rack to cool.

To make with a breadmaker

1 Coarsely grate the courgette and pat dry with kitchen paper.

2 Lift the tin out of the bread machine, fit the kneader blade then add the courgette, the measured cold water, olive oil, grated lemon rind and tarragon. Spoon in the flour then add the sugar, salt and a little pepper. Make a slight dip in the centre of the flour and sprinkle in the yeast (see page 14).

3 Insert the tin into the bread machine. Shut the lid and set to basic white/large 750 g (1½ lb) loaf/bake and select the preferred crust setting. Press start.

4 At the end of the programme, lift the tin out of the machine with oven gloves. Loosen the bread with a plastic spatula then turn out on to a wire rack and leave to cool.

Makes 1 large loaf

Tip If your bread machine does not have a setting for crust colour, you may find that the finished loaf is rather pale on top. To darken it, brush with a little butter and brown under the grill.

Feta and spinach twist

475 g (15 oz, 4⅓ cups) strong
white flour

2 teaspoons sugar

1¼ teaspoons salt

1¼ teaspoons fast-action dried
yeast

2 tablespoons olive oil

275 ml (9 fl oz, heaping 1 cup)
water

250 g (8 oz, 1 x 10-oz package)
frozen spinach, defrosted

a little grated nutmeg

150 g (5 oz, heaping ½ cup) feta
cheese, well drained

50 g (2 oz, ¼ cup) pine nuts

1 egg yolk, to glaze

salt and freshly ground black
pepper

To make by hand

1 Put the flour, sugar, salt and yeast into a large bowl.
Add the olive oil then gradually mix in enough warm
water to make a soft dough.

2 Knead well on a lightly floured surface for 5 minutes
until the dough is smooth and elastic. Put the dough
back into the bowl, cover loosely with oiled clingfilm
and leave in a warm place to rise for 1 hour or until
doubled in size.

3 Tip the dough out on to a lightly floured surface,
knead well then roll out to a 37.5 x 33 cm (15 x 13
inch) rectangle. Put the spinach into a sieve, press
out the liquid then sprinkle over the dough. Season
with salt, pepper and nutmeg, crumble over the feta
cheese and scatter over the pine nuts.

4 Roll up the dough, starting from the longest edge.
Brush the dough with the egg yolk mixed with
1 tablespoon of water then cut the dough in half
lengthways. Open out the pieces so that the cut
sides are uppermost, then press the ends together.
Loosely twist the two pieces together by lifting the
right hand piece over the left hand, then the first
piece back over the second until the ends are
reached (see page 19).

5 Carefully transfer the dough to a greased baking
sheet, tucking in any loose pieces of feta or nuts.
Leave to rise, uncovered, for 20–30 minutes.

6 Bake in a preheated oven, 200°C (400°F), Gas Mark
6, for 20–25 minutes until the bread is golden and
sounds hollow when tapped with the fingertips.
Check after 10 minutes and cover with foil if
overbrowning. Serve warm or cold.

To make with a breadmaker

1 Lift the tin out of the bread machine, fit the kneader
blade then add the measured cold water and oil.
Spoon over the flour, add the sugar and salt then
make a slight dip in the centre of the flour and
sprinkle in the yeast (see page 14).

2 Insert the tin into the bread machine, close the lid
and set to dough or basic dough. Press start.

3 Tip the dough out on to a lightly floured work surface.
Knead well then continue as step 3, left.

Makes 1 large loaf

Roasted red pepper and rosemary slippers

200 g (7 oz, 1¾ cups) strong
  white flour
250 g (8 oz, 2¼ cups) granary
  flour
1 tablespoon finely chopped
  rosemary
1½ teaspoons salt
1 teaspoon caster sugar
1¼ teaspoons fast-action dried
  yeast
2 tablespoons olive oil
250 ml (8 fl oz, 1 cup) water

FOR THE FILLING:

2 red peppers
1 yellow pepper
2 tablespoons olive oil
4 teaspoons balsamic vinegar
1 tablespoon sun-dried tomato
  paste
salt and freshly ground black
  pepper

TO FINISH:

2 tablespoons olive oil
fresh rosemary leaves

To make by hand

1 Put the flours into a large bowl then stir in the rosemary, salt, sugar and yeast. Add the oil and gradually mix in enough warm water to make a soft dough.

2 Knead well on a lightly floured surface for 5 minutes until the dough is smooth and elastic. Put back into the bowl, cover loosely with oiled clingfilm and leave in a warm place for 1 hour or until doubled in size.

3 Meanwhile, cut the peppers into quarters, removing the cores and seeds. Arrange on a grill rack with the skins uppermost and drizzle with the oil. Place under a preheated grill for 10 minutes until the skins are blackened. Wrap them in foil and leave to cool.

4 Remove the pepper skins with a small knife, then cut into thin strips. Season and toss with the vinegar.

5 Tip the dough out on to a lightly floured surface, knead well then cut in two. Roll each piece to a thin oval about 28 x 15 cm (11 x 6 inches). Spread with the tomato paste. Spoon half the peppers down the centre of each oval, then fold the dough in half lengthways to cover the mixture.

6 Carefully lift each loaf on to a large greased baking sheet. Sprinkle the tops with the remaining peppers then cover loosely with oiled clingfilm. Leave in a warm place for 30 minutes until well risen.

7 Remove the clingfilm and drizzle with oil and sprinkle with the extra rosemary. Bake in a preheated oven, 220°C (425°F), Gas Mark 7, for 15 minutes. Cover with foil if overbrowning. Serve hot or cold.

To make with a breadmaker

1 Lift the tin out of the bread machine, fit the kneader blade then add the measured cold water and oil. Spoon in the flour then add the rosemary, salt and sugar. Make a slight dip in the centre of the flour and sprinkle in the yeast (see page 14).

2 Insert the tin into the bread machine. Shut the lid and set to dough or basic dough. Press start.

3 Continue as step 3, left.

Makes 2 loaves

Tip If you plan to reheat this bread, slightly undercook it at first so it doesn't dry out when it is reheated.

Stuffed mushroom and garlic baguette

475 g (15 oz, 4⅓ cups) strong
white flour

1½ teaspoons sugar

1 teaspoon salt

1 teaspoon dried chilli seeds

2 teaspoons dried mixed herbes
de Provence

1¼ teaspoons fast-action dried
yeast

2 tablespoons olive oil

275 ml (9 fl oz, heaping 1 cup)
water

FILLING:

25 g (1 oz, 2 tablespoons) dried
sliced mixed mushrooms

150 ml (¼ pint, ⅔ cup) boiling
water

150 ml (¼ pint, ⅔ cup) red wine

2 tablespoons olive oil

1 red onion, chopped

2 garlic cloves, chopped

To make by hand

1 Put the flour into a large bowl then stir in the sugar, salt, chilli seeds, herbs and yeast. Add the oil and mix in enough warm water to make a soft dough.

2 Knead well until the dough is smooth and elastic. Put back into the bowl, cover with oiled clingfilm and leave to rise for 1 hour or until doubled in size.

3 Put the mushrooms in a bowl and pour over boiling water and red wine. Leave to soak for 30 minutes.

4 Heat half the oil in a frying pan, add the onion and garlic and fry for 5 minutes. Lift the mushrooms out of the soaking liquid, reserving the liquid. Set aside 2 tablespoons of the mushroom slices and 2 tablespoons of the fried onions for the topping.

5 Slice the other mushrooms, then add to the pan with the soaking liquid. Cook over a high heat for 3–5 minutes or until the liquid has almost boiled away.

6 Tip the dough out on to a lightly floured surface and knead well. Roll out to a rectangle about 43 x 23 cm (17 x 9 inches), spoon the mushroom mixture over the bread, in a thin layer, then roll up the dough starting with one of the longest edges.

7 Put the dough on a greased baking sheet, brush with oil and sprinkle with the reserved mushrooms and onion. Cover loosely with oiled clingfilm and leave in a warm place for 30 minutes until well risen.

8 Bake in a preheated oven, 200°C (400°F), Gas Mark 6, for 25–30 minutes until golden brown. Cover with foil if overbrowning. Transfer to a wire rack to cool.

To make with a breadmaker

1 Lift the tin out of the bread machine, fit the kneader blade then add the measured cold water and olive oil. Spoon in the flour then add the sugar, salt, chilli seeds and herbs. Make a slight dip in the centre of the flour then sprinkle in the yeast (see page 14).

2 Insert the tin into the bread machine. Shut the lid and set to dough or basic dough. Press start.

3 To make the filling and shape the bread continue as step 3, left.

Makes 1 loaf

Pesto, tomato and pine nut bread

475 g (15 oz, 4⅓ cups) strong
white flour

1½ teaspoons salt

2 teaspoons caster sugar

1¼ teaspoons fast-action dried
yeast

2 tablespoons olive oil

2 tablespoons pesto

275 ml (9 fl oz, heaping 1 cup)
water

75 g (3 oz, scant ½ cup)
sun-dried tomatoes (not in oil),
thinly sliced

3 tablespoons pine nuts

1 egg yolk, to glaze

To make by hand

1 Mix the flour, salt, sugar and yeast in a large bowl. Add the oil and pesto then gradually mix in enough warm water to make a soft dough.

2 Knead well on a lightly floured surface for 5 minutes until the dough is smooth and elastic. Work in the sun-dried tomatoes and all but 1 tablespoon of the pine nuts. Put the dough back into the bowl, cover loosely with oiled clingfilm and leave in a warm place to rise for 1 hour or until doubled in size.

3 Tip the dough out on to a lightly floured surface, knead well then press into a greased 18 cm (7 inch) deep square tin or 1 kg (2 lb) loaf tin.

4 Leave in a warm place to rise for 30 minutes or until the dough reaches the top of the tin.

5 Remove the clingfilm, brush with the egg yolk mixed with 1 tablespoon of water and sprinkle with the remaining pine nuts. Bake in a preheated oven, 200°C (400°F), Gas Mark 6, for 30–35 minutes until the bread is well risen and sounds hollow when tapped with the fingertips. Check after 15 minutes and cover with foil if overbrowning.

6 Holding the tin with oven gloves, loosen the bread with a palette knife. Transfer to a wire rack to cool.

To make with a breadmaker

1 Lift the tin out of the bread machine, fit the kneader blade then add the measured cold water, olive oil and pesto. Spoon in the flour then add the salt and sugar. Make a slight dip in the centre of the flour and sprinkle in the yeast (see page 14).

2 Insert the tin into the bread machine. Shut the lid and set to basic white/large 750 g (1½ lb) loaf/bake and select the preferred crust setting. Press start.

3 When the raisin beep sounds, add the sun-dried tomatoes and all but 1 tablespoon of the pine nuts. Shut the lid and allow the programme to continue.

4 About 1 hour before the end of the programme mix the egg yolk with 1 tablespoon of water and brush it over the top of the loaf. Sprinkle with the remaining pine nuts, shut the lid and allow the programme to continue.

5 At the end of the programme, lift the tin out of the machine with oven gloves. Loosen the bread with a plastic spatula then turn out on to a wire rack and leave to cool.

Makes 1 large loaf

Spiced potato and onion bread

A rich, golden crumb speckled with Indian-spiced onions, this moreish bread is delicious served warm with bowls of soup or lentil dahl.

200 g (7 oz, scant 1 cup) potato, peeled

1 tablespoon sunflower oil

150 g (5 oz, heaping 1 cup) onion, finely chopped

1½ teaspoons cumin seeds, roughly crushed

1½ teaspoons fennel seeds, roughly crushed

½ teaspoon turmeric

½ teaspoon paprika

2 tablespoons butter

475 g (15 oz, 4⅓ cups) strong white flour

2 teaspoons caster sugar

2 teaspoons salt

1½ teaspoons fast-action dried yeast

200 ml (7 fl oz, scant 1 cup) water

melted butter, to finish

To make by hand

1 Begin as steps 1 and 2, right.

2 Put the flour into a large bowl then stir in the sugar, salt and yeast. Add the potatoes, and all but 2 tablespoons of the spiced onions. Mix in enough warm water to make a soft dough.

3 Knead well on a lightly floured surface for 5 minutes until the dough is smooth and elastic. Put the dough back into the bowl, cover loosely with oiled clingfilm and leave in a warm place to rise for 1 hour or until doubled in size.

4 Tip the dough out on to a lightly floured surface, knead well then press into a greased 20 cm (8 inch) springform tin, mark into wedges and sprinkle with the reserved onions. Cover loosely with oiled clingfilm and leave for 30 minutes or until the dough reaches the top of the tin.

5 Remove the clingfilm and bake in a preheated oven, 200°C (400°F), Gas Mark 6, for 30–35 minutes until the bread is golden and sounds hollow when tapped with the fingertips.

6 Holding the tin with oven gloves, loosen the bread with a palette knife. Transfer to a wire rack and brush with a little extra melted butter and sprinkle with the reserved onion mixture.

To make with a breadmaker

1 Halve the potato then cook it in a small saucepan of boiling water for 15 minutes or until tender. Meanwhile, heat the oil in a frying pan, add the onion and fry gently until softened and pale golden. Stir in the spices and cook for 1 minute.

2 Drain the potato and mash finely with the butter. Leave to cool slightly.

3 Lift the tin out of the bread machine, fit the kneader blade then add the potato, all but 2 tablespoons of the spiced onions, and the measured cold water. Spoon in the flour then add the sugar and salt. Make a slight dip in the centre of the flour and sprinkle in the yeast (see page 14).

4 Insert the tin into the bread machine. Shut the lid and set to basic white/large 750 g (1½ lb) loaf/bake and select the preferred crust setting. Press start.

5 At the end of the programme, lift the tin out of the machine with oven gloves. Loosen the bread with a plastic spatula then turn out on to a wire rack. Brush with a little extra melted butter and sprinkle with the reserved onion mixture.

Makes 1 large loaf

Carrot and mustard bread

250 g (8 oz, 2¼ cups) malthouse or granary flour

200 g (7 oz, 1¾ cups) strong white flour

1½ teaspoons salt

2 tablespoons butter

1½ teaspoons fast-action dried yeast

1 tablespoon clear honey

2 tablespoons wholegrain mustard

125 g (4 oz, ½ cup) carrot, coarsely grated

200 ml (7 fl oz, scant 1 cup) water

1 egg yolk, to glaze

To make by hand

1 Put the flours and salt into a large bowl. Add the butter and rub in with the fingertips until the mixture resembles fine breadcrumbs. Add the yeast, honey, mustard and all the carrots then gradually mix in enough warm water to make a soft dough.

2 Knead well on a lightly floured surface for 5 minutes until the dough is smooth and elastic. Put the dough back into the bowl, cover loosely with oiled clingfilm and leave in a warm place to rise for 1 hour or until doubled in size.

3 Tip the dough out on to a lightly floured surface and knead well. Shape into a long rope about 50 cm (20 inches) in length. Twist several times (see page 19) then put into a greased 1.8 litre (3 pint) loaf tin.

4 Cover loosely with oiled clingfilm and leave in a warm place to rise for 30 minutes or until the dough reaches just above the top of the tin.

5 Remove the clingfilm, brush with the egg yolk mixed with 1 tablespoon of water and bake in a preheated oven, 200°C (400°F), Gas Mark 6, for 30–35 minutes until the bread is golden brown and sounds hollow when tapped with the fingertips. Check after 15 minutes and cover with foil if overbrowning.

6 Holding the tin with oven gloves, loosen the bread with a palette knife. Transfer to a wire rack to cool.

To make with a breadmaker

1 Lift the tin out of the bread machine, fit the kneader blade then add the measured cold water, butter, mustard, honey and half the carrot. Spoon in the flour then add the salt. Make a slight dip in the centre of the flour and sprinkle in the yeast (see page 14).

2 Insert the tin into the bread machine. Shut the lid and set to basic white/large 750 g (1½ lb) loaf/bake and select the preferred crust setting. Press start. When the raisin beep sounds, add the remaining carrots.

3 About 1 hour before the end of the programme mix the egg yolk with 1 tablespoon of water and brush it over the top of the dough. Shut the lid and continue with the programme.

4 At the end of the programme, lift the tin out of the machine with oven gloves. Loosen the bread with a plastic spatula then turn out on to a wire rack and leave to cool.

Makes 1 large loaf

Cheese and chutney corkscrew

475 g (15 oz, 4¼ cups) strong
   white flour

1 teaspoon caster sugar

1½ teaspoons salt

1½ teaspoons fast-action dried
   yeast

250 g (8 oz, 2 cups) mature
   Cheddar cheese, grated

6 spring onions, thickly sliced

2 tablespoons olive oil

250 ml (8 fl oz, 1 cup) water

6 tablespoons tomato chutney

1 egg yolk, to glaze

grated cheese, to garnish

To make by hand

1 Put the flour into a large bowl then stir in the sugar, salt and yeast. Mix in the cheese and onions then add the oil. Gradually mix in enough warm water to make a soft dough.

2 Knead well on a lightly floured surface for 5 minutes until the dough is smooth and elastic. Put the dough back into the bowl, cover loosely with oiled clingfilm and leave in a warm place to rise for about 1 hour or until doubled in size.

3 Tip the dough out on to a lightly floured surface, knead well then roll out to a large rectangle, about 46 x 25 cm (18 x 10 inches). Spread the chutney on in an even layer, almost up to the edges.

4 Starting with one of the longest edges, fold one-third of the dough towards the centre, then cover with the remaining third to make a strip about 46 x 10 cm (18 x 4 inches). Twist the folded dough 4 or 5 times to give a corkscrew effect then put on to a greased baking sheet.

5 Cover loosely with oiled clingfilm and leave in a warm place to rise for 30 minutes or until half as big again.

6 Remove the clingfilm and brush with the egg yolk mixed with 1 tablespoon of water. Sprinkle with a little extra grated cheese and bake in a preheated oven, 200°C (400°F), Gas Mark 6, for 30 minutes until the bread is well risen and golden and sounds hollow when tapped with the fingertips. Check after 10 minutes and cover with foil if overbrowning.

To make with a breadmaker

1 Lift the tin out of the bread machine, fit the kneader blade then add the measured cold water, oil, cheese and onions. Spoon the flour over the top then add the sugar and salt. Make a slight dip in the flour and sprinkle in the yeast (see page 14).

2 Insert the tin into the bread machine. Shut the lid and set the bread machine to dough only.

3 At the end of the programme, tip the dough out on to a floured surface and continue as step 3, left.

Makes 1 large loaf

Olive and tomato, tear and share bread

475 g (15 oz, 4⅓ cups) strong
   white flour

1 teaspoon salt

1 teaspoon caster sugar

1¼ teaspoons fast-action dried
   yeast

2 tablespoons olive oil

275 ml (9 fl oz, heaping 1 cup)
   water

125 g (4 oz, ½ cup) pitted or
   stuffed green olives, roughly
   chopped

40 g (1½ oz, 3 tablespoons)
   sun-dried tomatoes (not in oil),
   roughly chopped

coarse sea salt and paprika, to
   garnish

To make by hand

1 Put the flour, salt, sugar and yeast into a large bowl. Add the olive oil then gradually mix in enough warm water to make a soft dough.

2 Knead well on a lightly floured surface for 5 minutes until the dough is smooth and elastic. Put the dough back into the bowl, cover loosely with oiled clingfilm and leave in a warm place to rise for 1 hour or until doubled in size.

3 Tip the dough out on to a lightly floured surface and knead well. Gradually work in the chopped olives and tomatoes. Pat into a rough circle about 20 cm (8 inches) in diameter. Transfer to a greased baking sheet and mark the dough into 8 wedges, but do not cut right through to the base.

4 Sprinkle with the salt and paprika then cover loosely with oiled clingfilm and leave in a warm place to rise for 30 minutes or until half as big again.

5 Remove the clingfilm and bake in a preheated oven, 200°C (400°F), Gas Mark 6, for 30 minutes. Check after 15 minutes and cover with foil if overbrowning.

6 Holding the sheet with oven gloves, loosen the bread with a palette knife. Transfer to a wire rack and leave to cool.

To make with a breadmaker

1 Lift the tin out of the bread machine, fit the kneader blade then add the measured cold water and oil. Spoon in the flour then add the salt and sugar. Make a slight dip in the centre of the flour and sprinkle in the yeast (see page 14).

2 Insert the tin into the bread machine. Shut the lid and set to dough or basic dough. Press start.

3 At the end of the programme, lift the tin out of the machine, tip the dough out on to a lightly floured surface and continue as step 3, left.

Makes 1 large loaf

Tip The sun-dried tomatoes in this recipe are those packed in a dry cellophane bag. If you wish to use the kind preserved in oil, drain well and use double the quantity as the oil that has soaked into them makes them heavier.

4 sweet breads

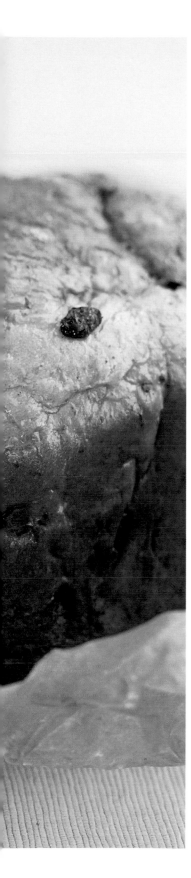

Banana and chocolate bread

300 g (10 oz, 1¼ cups) ripe banana, about 2 bananas weighed with skins on

2 teaspoons lemon juice

500 g (1 lb, 4½ cups) strong white flour

2 tablespoons milk powder

½ teaspoon salt

2 tablespoons caster sugar

2 tablespoons butter

1½ teaspoons fast-action dried yeast

200 ml (7 fl oz, scant 1 cup) water

175 g (6 oz) milk chocolate

icing sugar and cocoa powder, to decorate

To make by hand

1 Begin as step 1, right.

2 Put the flour, milk powder, salt and sugar into a large bowl. Add the butter and rub in with the fingertips until the mixture resembles fine breadcrumbs. Stir in the yeast and mashed bananas, then gradually mix in enough warm water to make a soft dough.

3 Knead well on a lightly floured surface for 5 minutes until the dough is smooth and elastic. Put the dough back into the bowl, cover loosely with oiled clingfilm and leave in a warm place to rise for 1 hour or until doubled in size.

4 Tip the dough out on to a lightly floured surface and knead well. Dice the chocolate then work it into the dough. Put the dough into a greased 1.8 litre (3 pint) loaf tin, cover loosely with oiled clingfilm and leave for 30 minutes or until the dough reaches the top of the tin.

5 Remove the clingfilm and bake in a preheated oven, 200°C (400°F), Gas Mark 6, for 35–40 minutes until the bread is golden brown and sounds hollow when tapped with the fingertips. Check after 20 minutes and cover with foil if overbrowning.

6 Holding the tin with oven gloves, loosen the bread with a palette knife. Transfer to a wire rack and dust with sifted icing sugar and cocoa. Leave to cool.

To make with a breadmaker

1 Peel the bananas and mash them on a plate with a fork, then work in the lemon juice.

2 Lift the tin out of the bread machine, fit the kneader blade then add the mashed bananas, measured cold water, milk powder and butter. Spoon in the flour then add the salt and sugar. Make a slight dip in the centre of the flour and sprinkle in the yeast (see page 14).

3 Insert the tin into the bread machine. Shut the lid and set to basic white/extra large 1 kg (2 lb) loaf/bake and select the preferred crust setting. Press start.

4 Dice the chocolate and add to the tin when the raisin beep sounds. Shut the lid and allow the programme to continue.

5 At the end of the programme, lift the tin out of the machine with oven gloves. Loosen the bread with a plastic spatula then turn out on to a wire rack. Dust with sifted icing sugar and cocoa and leave to cool completely.

Makes 1 extra large loaf

Spiced bubble bread

500 g (1 lb, 4½ cups) strong white flour

2 tablespoons butter

4 tablespoons (¼ cup) milk powder

1 teaspoon salt

75 g (3 oz, ⅓ cup) caster sugar

1¼ teaspoons fast-action dried yeast

300 ml (½ pint, 1¼ cups) water

1½ teaspoons ground cinnamon

½ teaspoon grated nutmeg

To make by hand

1 Put the flour into a large bowl, add the butter and rub in with the fingertips until the mixture resembles fine breadcrumbs. Stir in the milk powder, salt, 1 teaspoon of sugar and the yeast. Gradually mix in enough warm water to make a soft dough.

2 Knead well on a lightly floured surface for 5 minutes until the dough is smooth and elastic. Put back into the bowl, cover loosely with oiled clingfilm and leave in a warm place for 1 hour or until doubled in size.

3 Tip the dough out on to a lightly floured surface and knead well. Cut into 30 pieces and shape each piece into a small ball.

4 Mix the remaining sugar, cinnamon and nutmeg together in a shallow bowl. Roll the dough balls, one at a time, in the sugar mixture then arrange 14 in a greased 20 cm (8 inch) springform tin. Arrange a second layer, with the balls balanced over the spaces between the lower ones, rather like bricks in a wall.

5 Cover loosely with oiled clingfilm and leave in a warm place to rise for 30 minutes or until the dough just reaches above the top of the tin.

6 Remove the clingfilm and bake in a preheated oven, 200ºC (400ºF), Gas Mark 6, for 35 minutes. Check after 15 minutes and cover with foil if overbrowning.

7 Holding the tin with oven gloves, loosen the bread with a palette knife and transfer to a wire rack. Sprinkle with any remaining spiced sugar and leave to cool.

To make with a breadmaker

1 Lift the tin out of the bread machine, fit the kneader blade then add the measured cold water, butter and milk powder. Spoon in the flour then add the salt and 1 teaspoon of the sugar. Make a slight dip in the centre of the flour and sprinkle in the yeast (see page 14).

2 Insert the tin into the bread machine. Shut the lid and set to dough or basic dough. Press start.

3 At the end of the programme, lift the tin out of the machine and tip the dough out on to a lightly floured surface. Continue as step 3, left.

Makes 1 large loaf

Chocolate and pecan spiral

500 g (1 lb, 4½ cups) strong
    white flour
3 tablespoons butter
½ teaspoon salt
50 g (2 oz, ¼ cup) caster sugar
1½ teaspoon fast-action dried
    yeast
2 eggs, beaten
175 ml (6 fl oz, ¾ cup) milk

FILLING:

125 g (4 oz) plain dark
    chocolate, finely chopped
125 g (4 oz, ½ cup) pecan nuts,
    roughly chopped
2 tablespoons caster sugar
1 egg yolk, to glaze

To make by hand

1 Put the flour into a large bowl, add the butter and rub in with the fingertips until the mixture resembles fine breadcrumbs. Stir in the salt, sugar and yeast. Add the beaten eggs and gradually mix in enough warm milk to make a soft dough.

2 Knead well on a lightly floured surface for 5 minutes until the dough is smooth and elastic. Put the dough back into the bowl, cover loosely with oiled clingfilm and leave in a warm place to rise for 1 hour or until doubled in size.

3 Tip the dough out on to a lightly floured surface, knead well then roll out to a 27 cm (11 inch) square. Sprinkle with three quarters of the chocolate and nuts, and all the sugar.

4 Roll up the dough then put it into a greased 1.8 litre (3 pint) loaf tin. Cover loosely with oiled clingfilm and leave in a warm place for 30 minutes or until the dough reaches just above the top of the tin.

5 Remove the clingfilm, brush with the egg yolk mixed with 1 tablespoon of water and sprinkle with the remaining chocolate and pecan nuts. Bake in a preheated oven, 200°C (400°F), Gas Mark 6, for 35–40 minutes until the bread is well risen and deep brown and sounds hollow when tapped with the fingertips. Cover with foil after 10 minutes to prevent the nuts overbrowning.

6 Holding the tin with oven gloves, loosen the bread with a palette knife. Transfer to a wire rack to cool.

To make with a breadmaker

1 Lift the tin out of the bread machine, fit the kneader blade then add the milk, beaten eggs and butter. Spoon in the flour then add the salt and sugar. Make a slight dip in the centre of the flour and sprinkle in the yeast (see page 14).

2 Insert the tin into the bread machine. Shut the lid and set to dough or sweet dough. Press start.

3 At the end of the programme, lift the tin out of the machine, tip the dough out on to a lightly floured surface and continue as step 3, left.

Makes 1 extra large loaf

> **Tip** As this bread contains fresh milk and an egg, do not use the delay timer facility.

Saffron and sultana bread

¾ teaspoon saffron strands

3 tablespoons boiling water

475 g (15 oz, 4⅓ cups) strong
white flour

3 tablespoons butter

2 tablespoons milk powder

¼ teaspoon salt

¼ teaspoon ground cinnamon

75 g (3 oz, ⅓ cup) caster sugar

1¼ teaspoons fast-action dried
yeast

250 ml (8 fl oz, 1 cup) water

125 g (4 oz, ½ cup) sultanas

50 g (2 oz, ¼ cup) chopped
candied peel

TO GLAZE:

2 tablespoons milk

1 tablespoon caster sugar

To make by hand

1 Begin as step 1, right.

2 Put the flour into a large bowl, add the butter and rub in with the fingertips until the mixture resembles fine breadcrumbs. Stir in the milk powder, salt, cinnamon, sugar and yeast.

3 Add the saffron strands, soaking liquid and enough warm water to make a soft dough.

4 Knead well on a lightly floured surface for 5 minutes until the dough is smooth and elastic. Gradually knead in the sultanas and candied peel. Put the dough back into the bowl, cover loosely with oiled clingfilm and leave in a warm place to rise for 1 hour or until doubled in size.

5 Tip the dough out on to a lightly floured surface, knead well then shape into an oval and press into a greased 1.8 litre (3 pint) loaf tin. Cover loosely with oiled clingfilm and leave to rise for 30 minutes or until the dough reaches just above the top of the tin.

6 Remove the clingfilm and bake in a preheated oven, 200°C (400°F), Gas Mark 6, for 35–40 minutes. Cover with foil after 15 minutes to prevent overbrowning.

7 Holding the tin with oven gloves, loosen the bread with a palette knife. Transfer to a wire rack and to glaze, continue as step 5, right.

To make with a breadmaker

1 Put the saffron into a small bowl or mug and cover with the boiling water. Leave to soak for at least 15 minutes.

2 Lift the tin out of the bread machine, fit the kneader blade then add the saffron strands and soaking liquid, measured cold water, milk powder and butter. Spoon in the flour then add the cinnamon, salt and sugar. Make a slight dip in the centre of the flour and sprinkle in the yeast (see page 14).

3 Insert the tin into the bread machine. Shut the lid and set to basic white/extra large 1 kg (2 lb) loaf/bake and select medium crust. Press start.

4 When the raisin beep sounds, add the sultanas and candied peel. Shut the lid and allow the programme to continue.

5 At the end of the programme, lift the tin out of the machine with oven gloves. Loosen the bread with a plastic spatula then turn out on to a wire rack. Put the milk and sugar into a small saucepan, heat gently to dissolve the sugar then boil for 1 minute. Brush the glaze over the top of the hot bread and leave to cool.

Makes 1 extra large loaf

Yogurt, honey and fennel seed bread

Packed with all the flavours of the Greek islands, this irresistible loaf is delicious served simply spread with butter and apricot jam.

500 g (1 lb, 4½ cups) strong white flour

2 tablespoons butter

½ teaspoon salt

2 tablespoons fennel seeds, roughly crushed

1¼ teaspoon fast-action dried yeast

4 tablespoons (¼ cup) thick set honey

150 g (5 oz, heaping ½ cup) Greek yogurt

200 ml (7 fl oz, scant 1 cup) water

To make by hand

1 Put the flour into a large bowl. Add the butter and rub in until the mixture resembles fine breadcrumbs then stir in the salt, fennel seeds and yeast. Add the honey and yogurt then gradually mix in enough warm water to make a soft dough.

2 Knead on a lightly floured surface for 5 minutes until the dough is smooth and elastic. Put back into the bowl, cover loosely with oiled clingfilm and leave in a warm place to rise for 1 hour or until doubled in size.

3 Tip the dough out on to a lightly floured surface and knead well. Shape into a large round, put on to a greased baking sheet and make criss-cross cuts over the top. Cover loosely with oiled clingfilm and leave in a warm place for 45 minutes or until half as big again.

4 Remove the clingfilm, sprinkle with a little flour and bake in a preheated oven, 200°C (400°F), Gas Mark 6, for 30–35 minutes until the bread is well risen and golden and sounds hollow when tapped with the fingertips. Check after 15 minutes and cover with foil if overbrowning.

5 Holding the sheet with oven gloves, loosen the bread with a palette knife. Transfer to a wire rack to cool.

To make with a breadmaker

1 Lift the tin out of the bread machine, fit the kneader blade then add the measured cold water, yogurt, butter and honey. Spoon in the flour then add the salt and fennel seeds. Make a slight dip in the centre of the flour and sprinkle in the yeast (see page 14).

2 Insert the tin into the bread machine. Shut the lid and set to basic white/extra large 1 kg (2 lb) loaf/bake and select the preferred crust setting. Press start.

3 At the end of the programme, lift the tin out of the machine with oven gloves. Loosen the bread with a plastic spatula then turn out on to a wire rack and leave to cool.

Makes 1 extra large loaf

Gingered fig and orange bread

1 large orange, freshly squeezed or 200 ml (7 fl oz, scant 1 cup) fresh, shop-bought orange juice

150 g (5 oz, heaping ½ cup) dried figs, chopped

175 g (6 oz, 1½ cups) strong wholemeal flour

300 g (10 oz, 2⅔ cups) strong white flour

2 tablespoons butter

1 teaspoon salt

1¼ teaspoons fast-action dried yeast

4 tablespoons (¼ cup) thick set honey

150 ml (¼ pint, ⅔ cup) water

4 teaspoons chopped glacé or candied ginger

milk, to glaze

To make by hand

1 Begin as step 1, right.

2 Put the flours into a large bowl, add the butter and rub in with the fingertips until the mixture resembles fine breadcrumbs. Stir in the salt and yeast then add the honey. Drain the orange juice and add to the bowl then gradually mix in enough warm water to make a soft dough.

3 Knead well on a lightly floured surface for 5 minutes until the dough is smooth and elastic. Gradually work in the soaked figs and the ginger. Put the dough back into the bowl, cover loosely with oiled clingfilm and leave in a warm place to rise for 1 hour or until doubled in size.

4 Tip the dough out on to a lightly floured surface, knead well then shape into an oval and press into a greased 1.8 litre (3 pint) loaf tin. Cover loosely with oiled clingfilm and leave in a warm place to rise for 30 minutes or until the dough reaches just above the top of the tin.

5 Remove the clingfilm, brush with milk and bake in a preheated oven, 200°C (400°F), Gas Mark 6, for 35–40 minutes until the bread is well risen, deep brown in colour and sounds hollow when tapped with the fingertips. Cover with foil after 15 minutes to prevent overbrowning.

6 Holding the tin with oven gloves, loosen the bread with a palette knife. Transfer to a wire rack to cool.

To make with a breadmaker

1 Warm the orange juice in a small saucepan, add the chopped figs and set aside for 30 minutes.

2 Lift the tin out of the bread machine, fit the kneader blade then add the strained orange juice with half the soaked figs, the measured cold water, honey and butter. Spoon in the flours and salt. Make a slight dip in the centre of the flours and sprinkle in the yeast (see page 14).

3 Insert the tin into the bread machine. Shut the lid and set to basic white/extra large 1 kg (2 lb) loaf/bake and select the preferred crust setting. Press start.

4 After 20–30 minutes or when the raisin beep sounds, add the remaining figs and the ginger. Run a plastic spatula around the edge of the tin to make sure they mix in fully. Shut the lid and allow the programme to continue.

5 At the end of the programme, lift the tin out of the machine using oven gloves. Loosen the bread with a plastic spatula then turn out on to a wire rack and leave to cool.

Makes 1 extra large loaf

Sticky malt and raisin loaf

Full of malty flavour, this light, moist, raisin-peppered bread makes a great teatime treat spread with butter and thick honey or toasted for breakfast the following day.

425 g (14 oz, 3¾ cups)
   unbleached strong white flour
2 tablespoons soft light brown
   sugar
2 tablespoons milk powder
1 teaspoon salt
1¼ teaspoons fast-action dried
   yeast
3 tablespoons barley malt extract
2 tablespoons sunflower oil
2 teaspoons treacle
200 ml (7 fl oz, scant 1 cup)
   water
125 g (4 oz, ½ cup) raisins

TO GLAZE:
2 tablespoons milk
1 tablespoon caster sugar

To make by hand

1 Mix the flour, sugar, milk powder, salt and yeast in a large bowl. Add the malt extract, oil and treacle. Gradually mix in enough warm water to make a soft dough.

2 Knead well on a lightly floured surface for 5 minutes until the dough is smooth and elastic. Gradually knead in the raisins, then put the dough back into the bowl. Cover loosely with oiled clingfilm and leave in a warm place to rise for 1 hour or until doubled in size.

3 Tip the dough out on to a lightly floured surface, knead well then press into a greased 1 kg (2 lb) loaf tin.

4 Cover loosely with oiled clingfilm and leave in a warm place to rise for 30 minutes or until the dough reaches just above the top of the tin.

5 Remove the clingfilm and bake in a preheated oven, 200°C (400°F), Gas Mark 6, for 30–35 minutes until the bread is well risen, browned and sounds hollow when tapped with the fingertips. Check after 15 minutes and cover with foil if overbrowning.

6 Holding the tin with oven gloves, loosen the bread with a palette knife. Transfer to a wire rack and to glaze, continue as step 4, right.

To make with a breadmaker

1 Lift the tin out of the bread machine, fit the kneader blade then add the measured cold water, malt extract, sugar, oil, milk powder, treacle and salt. Spoon in the flour. Make a slight dip in the centre of the flour and sprinkle in the yeast (see page 14).

2 Insert the tin into the bread machine. Shut the lid and set to basic white/large 750 g (1½ lb) loaf/bake and select the preferred crust setting. Press start.

3 After 20 minutes or when the raisin beep sounds, add the raisins, shut the lid and allow the programme to continue.

4 At the end of the programme, lift the tin out of the machine with oven gloves. Loosen with a plastic spatula then turn out on to a wire rack. Put the milk and sugar into a small saucepan, heat gently to dissolve the sugar then boil for 1 minute. Brush over the top and sides of the hot bread and leave to cool.

Makes 1 large loaf

> **Tip** If the top of the bread does not seem very brown when you take the loaf out of the bread machine, brown it a little more under the grill and then brush with the glaze.

Kugelhopf

An Austrian favourite, this rich, buttery bread is flecked with boozy, soaked fruits and baked. A tall, crownlike mould gives it its distinctive shape.

3 tablespoons Kirsch, rum or
brandy
150 g (5 oz, heaping ½ cup)
mixed dried fruit
400 g (13 oz, 3⅔ cups) strong
white flour
75 g (3 oz, ⅓ cup) caster sugar
½ teaspoon salt
½ teaspoon ground cinnamon
1 large orange, grated rind only
2 teaspoons fast-action dried
yeast
75 g (3 oz, ¼ cup plus 2
tablespoons) butter, melted
3 eggs, beaten
150 ml (¼ pint, ⅔ cup) milk
semolina or fine dried
breadcrumbs, to line tin

To make by hand

1 Begin as step 1, right.

2 Put the flour, sugar, salt, cinnamon, orange rind and yeast into a large bowl. Add the melted butter and beaten eggs then gradually beat in the warmed milk to make a thick batter.

3 Cover the top of the bowl loosely with oiled clingfilm and leave in a warm place to rise for 1 hour or until doubled in size.

4 Brush the inside of a 2.5 litre (4 pint) kugelhopf tin or fluted ring mould tin with sunflower oil then sprinkle with semolina or breadcrumbs. Beat the soaked fruit and spirit into the risen mixture then pour into the prepared tin.

5 Cover the top of the tin loosely with oiled clingfilm and leave in a warm place to rise for 45 minutes or until the mixture just reaches the top of the tin.

6 Remove the clingfilm and bake in a preheated oven, 190°C (375°F), Gas Mark 5, for 35–40 minutes. Check after 20 minutes and cover with foil if overbrowning.

7 Leave the bread to stand in the tin for 5 minutes, then loosen the edges and centre with a small knife. Transfer to a wire rack to cool.

To make in a breadmaker

1 Warm the spirit in a small saucepan then add the dried fruit and leave to soak for 2 hours.

2 Lift the tin out of the bread machine, fit the kneader blade then add the milk, melted butter and beaten eggs. Spoon in the flour, sugar, salt, cinnamon and orange rind. Make a slight dip in the centre of the flour and sprinkle in the yeast (see page 14).

3 Insert the tin into the bread machine. Shut the lid and set to dough or enriched dough. Press start.

4 At the end of the programme, lift the tin out of the machine and continue as step 4, left.

Makes 1 loaf

Tips As this bread contains fresh milk, butter and eggs, do not use the delay timer facility.

Specialist flexible kugelhopf moulds or standard metal kugelhopf tins can be bought in good cookshops. Alternatively, use a 23 cm (9 inch) springform tin with a ring mould inset. Always brush metal tins with oil so that the bread does not stick.

Nectarine and marzipan fruit küchen

This German-inspired lemon bread is topped with grated marzipan and thick slices of ripe nectarine. Baked in a tart tin, it is a cross between a sweet pizza and a bread-based tart tatin.

300 g (10 oz, 2⅔ cups) strong
  white flour
2 tablespoons butter
¼ teaspoon salt
25 g (1 oz, 2 tablespoons) caster
  sugar
1 tablespoon milk powder
1 lemon, grated rind only
¾ teaspoon fast-action dried
  yeast
1 egg, beaten
150 ml (¼ pint, ⅔ cup) water

FOR THE TOPPING:
125 g (4 oz, ½ cup) ready-made
  marzipan, coarsely grated
500 g (1 lb) ripe nectarines
25 g (1 oz, 2 tablespoons) butter,
  melted
2 tablespoons caster sugar

TO DECORATE:
toasted flaked almonds
extra caster sugar

To make by hand

1 Put the flour into a large bowl, add the butter and rub in with fingertips until the mixture resembles fine breadcrumbs. Stir in the salt, sugar, milk powder, lemon rind and yeast. Add the beaten egg and enough warm water to make a soft dough.

2 Knead well on a lightly floured surface for 5 minutes until the dough is smooth and elastic. Put the dough back into the bowl, cover loosely with oiled clingfilm and leave in a warm place to rise for 1 hour or until doubled in size.

3 Tip the dough out on to a lightly floured surface, knead well then press into a buttered 28 cm (11 inch) fluted loose-bottomed flan tin.

4 Sprinkle with the grated marzipan. Halve, stone and thickly slice the nectarines and arrange them over the top. Leave to rise, uncovered, in a warm place for 40 minutes or until half as big again.

5 Brush the fruit with melted butter, sprinkle with sugar and bake in a preheated oven, 200°C (400°F), Gas Mark 6, for 15 minutes. Cover with foil, reduce heat to 180°C (350°F), Gas Mark 4, and bake for a further 35–40 minutes until the base is cooked through.

6 Leave to stand in the tin for 10 minutes, then loosen the edges and remove the tart from the tin, keeping it on the base. Transfer to a serving plate, sprinkle with flaked almonds and dust with extra sugar. Serve warm or cold cut into slices.

To make with a breadmaker

1 Lift the tin out of the bread machine, fit the kneader blade then add the measured cold water, beaten egg, butter and milk powder. Spoon in the flour, salt, sugar and lemon rind. Make a slight dip in the centre of the flour and sprinkle in the yeast (see page 14).

2 Insert the tin into the bread machine. Shut the lid and set to dough or basic dough. Press start.

3 At the end of the programme, lift the tin out of the machine, tip the dough out on to a lightly floured surface and continue as step 3, left.

Makes 1 large loaf (serves 6–8)

Tip If preferred, try using ripe peaches, apricots or plums for the topping.

Spiced pumpkin and sunflower seed bread

200 g (7 oz, scant 1 cup)
   pumpkin flesh, diced

1 teaspoon sunflower oil

4 tablespoons (¼ cup) sunflower
   seeds

400 g (13 oz, 3⅔ cups) strong
   coarse wholemeal flour

2 tablespoons butter

3 tablespoons soft light brown
   sugar

1 teaspoon ground cinnamon

1 teaspoon ground ginger

½ teaspoon grated nutmeg

½ teaspoon salt

1¼ teaspoons fast-action dried
   yeast

4 tablespoons (¼ cup) maple
   syrup

200 ml (7 fl oz, scant 1 cup)
   water

milk, to glaze

To make by hand

1 Begin as steps 1 and 2, right.

2 Put the flour into a large bowl, add the butter and rub in with the fingertips until the mixture resembles fine breadcrumbs. Stir in the sugar, spices, salt and yeast. Add the maple syrup and three quarters of the toasted seeds then gradually mix in enough warm water to make a soft dough.

3 Knead well on a lightly floured surface for 5 minutes until the dough is smooth and elastic. Put the dough back into the bowl, cover loosely with oiled clingfilm and leave in a warm place to rise for 1 hour or until doubled in size.

4 Tip the dough out on to a lightly floured surface, knead well then gradually work in the steamed pumpkin, adding a little extra flour if the dough becomes sticky. Shape into a round about 18 cm (7 inches) in diameter. Transfer to a greased baking sheet.

5 Cover loosely with oiled clingfilm and leave in a warm place to rise for 30 minutes or until half as big again.

6 Remove the clingfilm and make a cross cut in the top of the dough. Brush with milk then sprinkle with the reserved seeds. Bake in a preheated oven, 200°C (400°F), Gas Mark 6, for 25–30 minutes until the bread is browned and sounds hollow when tapped with the fingertips. Check after 10 minutes and cover with foil if the seeds are overbrowning.

7 Holding the sheet with oven gloves, loosen the bread with a palette knife. Transfer to a wire rack to cool.

To make with a breadmaker

1 Put the diced pumpkin into the top of a steamer set over a saucepan of boiling water, cover and steam for 8–10 minutes until tender.

2 Put the oil into a small saucepan, add the sunflower seeds and fry for 2–3 minutes, stirring until browned.

3 Lift the tin out of the bread machine, fit the kneader blade then add the measured cold water, maple syrup, sugar and butter. Spoon in three-quarters of the toasted seeds, all the ground spices and salt. Add the flour then make a slight dip in the centre of the flour and sprinkle in the yeast (see page 14).

4 Insert the tin into the bread machine. Shut the lid and set to dough or basic dough. Press start.

5 At the end of the programme, lift the tin out of the machine, tip the dough out on to a lightly floured surface and continue as step 4, left.

Makes 1 large loaf

Tip If pumpkin is out of season, squash can be used instead, but always weigh the flesh after the skin and seeds have been removed.

flat breads

Spinach and pancetta pizzas

Try these garlicky spinach and Italian ham pizzas for a light lunch or supper, a pleasant change from the more usual tomato and cheese.

400 g (13 oz, 3⅔ cups) strong
    white flour
1 teaspoon salt
1 teaspoon caster sugar
1¼ teaspoons fast-action dried
    yeast
3 tablespoons olive oil
200 ml (7 fl oz, scant 1 cup)
    water

FOR THE TOPPING:
200 g (7 oz, scant 1 cup) canned
    chopped tomatoes
2 garlic cloves, chopped
50 g (2 oz, 2 cups) baby spinach
    leaves, well washed
400 g (7 oz) mozzarella cheese,
    drained and thinly sliced
50 g (2 oz, ¼ cup) sun-dried
    tomatoes (in oil), thinly sliced
100 g (3½ oz, ½ cup) pancetta,
    diced
2 tablespoons olive oil
salt and pepper

To make by hand

1 Put the flour into a large bowl then stir in the salt, sugar and yeast. Add the oil then gradually mix in enough warm water to make a soft dough.

2 Knead well on a lightly floured surface for 5 minutes until the dough is smooth and elastic. Put the dough back into the bowl, cover loosely with oiled clingfilm and leave in a warm place to rise for 1 hour or until doubled in size.

3 Tip the dough out on to a lightly floured surface, knead well then cut into 4 pieces. Roll each piece into a roughly shaped circle about 20 cm (8 inches) in diameter and transfer to 2 large greased baking sheets.

4 Spread the tops with the canned tomatoes to about 1 cm (½ inch) from the edge of the dough. Sprinkle with the garlic and salt and pepper. Arrange the spinach on the tomatoes, then tuck the mozzarella between the leaves. Top with sun-dried tomatoes, pancetta, extra salt and pepper and oil then leave in a warm place for 30 minutes or until the dough is risen around the edges.

5 Bake in a preheated oven, 220°C (425°F), Gas Mark 7, for 8–10 minutes or until the cheese is bubbling and the edges of the pizza are browned. Transfer to plates and serve immediately.

To make with a breadmaker

1 Lift the tin out of the bread machine, fit the kneader blade then add the measured cold water and oil. Spoon in the flour then add the salt and sugar. Make a slight dip in the centre of the flour and sprinkle in the yeast (see page 14).

2 Insert the tin into the bread machine. Shut the lid and set to dough or pizza dough. Press start.

3 At the end of the programme, lift the tin out of the machine, tip the dough out on to a lightly floured surface and continue as step 3, left.

Makes 4 x 20 cm (8 inch) pizzas

> **Tip** If you are making the pizzas by hand and are short of time, knead the dough for 10 minutes and miss out the first proving. Just shape, top, rise and then bake.

Pissaladière

This famous French onion and olive tart is topped with a lattice of anchovy fillets and has a thin bread base instead of pastry.

250 g (8 oz, 2¼ cups) strong
   white flour

½ teaspoon salt

1 teaspoon caster sugar

¾ teaspoon fast-action dried yeast

4 teaspoons olive oil

150 ml (¼ pint, ⅔ cup) water

FOR THE TOPPING:

3 tablespoons olive oil

500 g (1 lb) large onions, thinly
   sliced

1 teaspoon caster sugar

3 garlic cloves, crushed

few stems fresh thyme

50 g (2 oz, ¼ cup) canned
   anchovy fillets, drained, halved
   lengthways

75 g (3 oz, ⅓ cup) pitted black
   olives

salt and pepper

To make by hand

1 Put the flour into a large bowl then stir in the salt, sugar and yeast. Add the oil then gradually mix in enough warm water to make a soft dough.

2 Knead well on a lightly floured surface for 5 minutes until the dough is smooth and elastic. Put the dough back into the bowl, cover loosely with oiled clingfilm and leave in a warm place to rise for 45 minutes or until doubled in size.

3 Meanwhile, heat the oil in a frying pan, add the onions and fry gently for 15 minutes, stirring occasionally, until softened. Stir in the sugar and garlic and increase the heat. Fry for 5 more minutes, stirring frequently, until the onions are browned. Set aside.

4 Tip the dough out on to a lightly floured surface and knead well. Roll out to a rough rectangle then press into a greased 25 x 37 cm (10 x 15 inch) shallow baking tin, until the dough reaches the edges of the tin.

5 Pull the leaves off the thyme and stir into the onions with the salt and pepper. Spoon over the bread base and spread into an even layer, leaving a narrow border of dough at the edges. Make a lattice pattern over the onions with the halved anchovy fillets and fill in each hole with an olive. Leave in a warm place for 30 minutes or until the edges of the dough look puffy.

6 Bake in a preheated oven, 220°C (425°F), Gas Mark 7, for 12–15 minutes or until the edges are golden.

To make with a breadmaker

1 Lift the tin out of the bread machine, fit the kneader blade then add the measured cold water and oil. Spoon in the flour then add the salt and sugar. Make a slight dip in the centre of the flour and sprinkle in the yeast (see page 14).

2 Insert the tin into the bread machine. Shut the lid and set to dough or pizza dough. Press start.

3 To make the topping and shape the dough, continue as step 3, left.

Makes 1 large tart (serves 4)

Tip In place of thyme leaves, try rosemary, basil or oregano, if preferred.

Buttered garlic and basil sticks

400 g (13 oz, 3⅔ cups) strong
   white flour
1 teaspoon salt
1 teaspoon caster sugar
1¼ teaspoons fast-action dried
   yeast
2 tablespoons olive oil
200 ml (7 fl oz, scant 1 cup)
   water
coarse sea salt

TO FINISH:
100 g (3½ oz, ¾ cup plus 1
   tablespoon) butter
4 garlic cloves, finely chopped
1 small bunch fresh basil
pepper

To make by hand

1 Put the flour into a large bowl then stir in the salt, sugar and yeast. Add the olive oil then gradually mix in enough warm water to make a soft dough.

2 Knead well on a lightly floured surface for 5 minutes until the dough is smooth and elastic. Put the dough back into the bowl, cover loosely with oiled clingfilm and leave in a warm place to rise for 1 hour or until doubled in size.

3 Tip the dough out on to a lightly floured surface, knead well then cut in half. Roll each half out to a thin oval about 35 x 18 cm (14 x 7 inches). Transfer to 2 greased baking sheets and cut into 2.5 cm (1 inch) strips, making cuts a little in from the edge of the dough so that strips are still held together at the ends within the oval shape.

4 Sprinkle the dough with a little coarse salt. Cover loosely with oiled clingfilm and leave in a warm place for 30 minutes until the bread has risen around the edges.

5 Remove the clingfilm and bake in a preheated oven, 220°C (425°F), Gas Mark 7, for 8–10 minutes until the bread is golden and sounds hollow when tapped with the fingertips. Transfer to 2 large plates.

6 Melt a small piece of butter in a saucepan and add the garlic. Fry for 2–3 minutes until just beginning to brown. Add the remaining butter, basil leaves torn into pieces and black pepper to taste. When the butter has melted, brush this over the hot bread, separate into sticks and serve immediately.

To make with a breadmaker

1 Lift the tin out of the bread machine, fit the kneader blade then add the measured cold water and oil. Spoon in the flour then add the salt and sugar. Make a slight dip in the centre of the flour and sprinkle in the yeast (see page 14).

2 Insert the tin into the bread machine. Shut the lid and set to dough or basic dough. Press start.

3 At the end of the programme, lift the tin out of the machine, tip the dough on to a lightly floured surface and continue as step 3, left.

Makes about 20 sticks

Tip To make these breadsticks in advance, brush the hot breads thinly with a little of the butter mixture, then leave to cool completely on a wire rack. Warm them when needed and brush with the remaining warmed butter when ready to serve.

Grissini

These crisp Italian breadsticks are usually served with drinks or antipasta – a mixed platter of olives, sliced salami, Parma ham and other mixed meats, marinated peppers, artichoke hearts and other salads.

475 g (15 oz, 4⅓ cups) strong white flour

1½ teaspoons sugar

1 teaspoon salt

1¼ teaspoons fast-action dried yeast

3 tablespoons olive oil

275 ml (9 fl oz, 1 cup plus 2 tablespoons) water

5 teaspoons sesame seeds

2 teaspoons fennel seeds

1 tablespoon fresh chopped rosemary, basil or chives

1 egg yolk, to glaze

1 teaspoon salt flakes

To make by hand

1 Put the flour into a large bowl then stir in the sugar, salt and yeast. Add the oil then gradually mix in enough warm water to make a soft dough.

2 Knead well on a lightly floured surface for 5 minutes until the dough is smooth and elastic. Put the dough back into the bowl, cover loosely with lightly oiled clingfilm and leave in a warm place to rise for 1 hour or until doubled in size.

3 Tip the dough out on to a lightly floured surface and knead well. Cut into 4 pieces. Leave one quarter plain, knead the sesame seeds into the second piece, the fennel seeds into the third piece and the chopped herbs into the last piece. Cut each quarter into 8 pieces, then roll each piece into a long rope about 25 cm (10 inches) long. Transfer to 2 large greased baking sheets.

4 Cover loosely with oiled clingfilm and leave in a warm place for 30 minutes or until the dough is well risen.

5 Remove the clingfilm and brush the breadsticks with the egg yolk mixed with 1 tablespoon of water. Sprinkle the plain ones with the salt. Bake in a preheated oven, 200°C (400°F), Gas Mark 6, for 6–8 minutes or until golden.

6 Holding the sheets with oven gloves, loosen the breadsticks with a palette knife. Transfer to a wire rack to cool.

To make with a breadmaker

1 Lift the tin out of the bread machine, fit the kneader blade then add the measured cold water and oil. Spoon in the flour, then add the salt and sugar. Make a slight dip in the flour and sprinkle in the yeast (see page 14).

2 Insert the tin into the bread machine. Shut the lid and set to dough or basic dough only. Press start.

3 At the end of the programme, lift the tin out of the bread machine and tip the dough out on to a lightly floured work surface. Continue as step 3, left.

Makes 32 sticks

Pitta bread

These soft flat breads puff up during baking to make a pouch and are ideal for filling with grilled meats or vegetables, or cut into strips and served with dips.

375 g (12 oz, 3½ cups) strong
  white flour
1 teaspoon salt
1 teaspoon caster sugar
1½ teaspoons fast-action dried
  yeast
1 tablespoon olive oil
250 ml (8 fl oz, 1 cup) water

To make by hand

1 Put the flour into a large bowl then stir in the salt, sugar and yeast. Add the oil then gradually mix in enough warm water to make a soft dough.

2 Knead well on a lightly floured surface for 5 minutes until the dough is smooth and elastic. Put the dough back into the bowl, cover loosely with oiled clingfilm and leave in a warm place to rise for 1 hour or until doubled in size.

3 Tip the dough out on to a lightly floured surface, knead well then cut into 8 pieces. Roll out the pieces into ovals of about 15 cm (6 inches) or into ovals a little smaller than your hand.

4 Put the dough on to pieces of oiled clingfilm and cover loosely with more oiled clingfilm. Leave to rise for 15 minutes.

5 Heat 3 baking sheets in a preheated oven, 220°C (425°F), Gas Mark 7, for 5–7 minutes. Rinse the trays with cold water so that the breads won't stick then quickly put the breads on the hot baking trays and cook for 6–8 minutes until puffy and just beginning to brown.

6 Serve the pitta breads warm or wrap them in a clean tea towel to keep them soft and leave to cool on a wire rack. To serve, slit open and stuff the pockets with fillings.

To make with a breadmaker

1 Lift the tin out of the bread machine, fit the kneader blade then add the measured cold water and oil. Spoon in the flour then add the salt and sugar. Make a slight dip in the centre of the flour and sprinkle in the yeast (see page 14).

2 Insert the tin into the bread machine. Shut the lid and set to dough or basic dough. Press start.

3 At the end of the programme, lift the tin out of the machine, tip the dough out on to a lightly floured surface and continue as step 3, left.

Makes 8

Tip To reheat the breads, sprinkle with a little water and cook under a hot grill for 1 minute on each side.

Tomato focaccia

475 g (15 oz, 4⅓ cups) strong
   white flour
1 teaspoon sugar
1 teaspoon salt
1½ teaspoons fast-action dried
   yeast
3 tablespoons olive oil
275 ml (9 fl oz, heaping 1 cup)
   water

FOR THE TOPPING:
200 g (7 oz, scant 1 cup) cherry
   tomatoes
a few sprigs of rosemary
a few black olives
1 teaspoon salt flakes
3 tablespoons olive oil

To make by hand

1 Put the flour, sugar, salt and yeast into a large bowl. Add the olive oil then gradually mix in enough warm water to make a soft dough.

2 Knead the dough well on a lightly floured surface for 5 minutes until it is smooth and elastic. Put the dough back into the bowl, cover loosely with oiled clingfilm and leave in a warm place to rise for 1 hour or until doubled in size.

3 Tip the dough out on to a lightly floured surface, knead well then cut into 2 pieces. Press each into a rough oval shape a little larger than your hand.

4 Transfer the loaves to 2 greased baking sheets then make indentations in the surface of each bread with the end of a wooden spoon. Remove the green tops from the tomatoes and press the tomatoes into some of the indentations, add small sprigs of rosemary and olives to some of the others. Sprinkle with the salt flakes and leave to rise, uncovered, for 20 minutes.

5 Drizzle the loaves with a little of the oil and bake in a preheated oven, 200°C (400°F), Gas Mark 6, for 15 minutes. Swap shelf positions during cooking, so that they both brown evenly. Drizzle with the remaining olive oil and serve warm or cold, torn into pieces.

To make with a breadmaker

1 Lift the tin out of the bread machine, fit the kneader blade then add the measured cold water and oil. Spoon in the flour then add the sugar and salt. Make a slight dip in the centre of the flour and sprinkle in the yeast (see page 14).

2 Insert the tin into the bread machine. Shut the lid and set to dough or basic dough. Press start.

3 At the end of the programme, lift the tin out of the machine, tip the dough out on to a lightly floured surface and continue as step 3, left.

Makes 2 loaves

Naan bread

Traditionally cooked on the sides of a tandoor oven, these flat Indian breads can be successfully made at home by cooking them on a heated griddle or in heavy frying pan.

500 g (1 lb, 4½ cups) strong
    white flour

2 teaspoons caster sugar

1½ teaspoons salt

2 teaspoons cumin seeds

2 teaspoons black mustard or
    onion seeds

3 tablespoons fresh chopped
    coriander leaves

1¼ teaspoons fast-action dried
    yeast

2 tablespoons butter, melted

150 ml (¼ pint, ⅔ cup) natural
    yogurt

150 ml (¼ pint, ⅔ cup) milk

3 tablespoons water

1 tablespoon sunflower oil

To make by hand

1 Put the flour into a large bowl then stir in the sugar, salt, seeds, coriander leaves and yeast. Add the butter, yogurt and warmed milk then gradually mix in enough warm water to make a soft dough.

2 Knead well on a lightly floured surface for 5 minutes until the dough is smooth and elastic. Put the dough back into the bowl, cover loosely with oiled clingfilm and leave in a warm place to rise for 1¼ hours or until doubled in size.

3 Tip the dough out on to a lightly floured surface and knead well. Cut into 6 pieces then roll each piece out to an oval a little larger than your hand.

4 Put the breads on to pieces of oiled clingfilm and then cover loosely with more oiled clingfilm. Leave in a warm place to rise for 20 minutes or until puffy around the edges.

5 Meanwhile, oil and heat a griddle or heavy-based frying pan. Add as many naan bread as will fit comfortably (see page 22) and cook for 5 minutes, turning once, until browned and cooked through. Cook the remaining breads in the same way.

To make with a breadmaker

1 Lift the tin out of the bread machine, fit the kneader blade then add the milk, yogurt, measured cold water and melted butter. Spoon in the flour then add the salt, sugar, seeds and coriander leaves. Make a slight dip in the centre of the flour and sprinkle in the yeast (see page 14).

2 Insert the tin into the bread machine. Shut the lid and set to dough or basic dough. Press start.

3 At the end of the programme, lift the tin out of the machine, tip the dough out on to a lightly floured surface. Continue as step 3, left.

Makes 6

Tip As this bread contains fresh milk and yogurt, do not use the delay timer facility.

Mosaic bread

400 g (13 oz, 3⅔ cups)
   unbleached strong white flour
1 teaspoon salt
2 teaspoons sugar
1¼ teaspoons fast-action dried
   yeast
250 ml (8 fl oz, 1 cup) water

TO BAKE ON:
12 pebbles, around 7–10 cm
   (3–4 inches), or enough to
   cover the bottom of your oven

To make by hand

1 Mix the flour, salt, sugar and yeast in a large bowl. Gradually mix in enough warm water to make a soft dough.

2 Knead well on a lightly floured surface for 5 minutes until the dough is smooth and elastic. Put the dough back into the bowl, cover loosely with oiled clingfilm and leave in a warm place to rise for 1 hour or until doubled in size.

3 Meanwhile, scrub the pebbles in a bowl of hot soapy water. Rinse well with hot water and drain.

4 Take the shelves out of the oven and then preheat it to 200°C (400°F), Gas Mark 6. Arrange the pebbles on the base of the oven and heat for 40 minutes.

5 Tip the dough out on to a lightly floured surface, knead well then cut into 4 pieces. Roll each piece into a rough 20 cm (8 inch) circle, transfer to 2 large greased baking sheets and cover loosely with oiled clingfilm. Leave in a warm place to rise for 30 minutes or until puffy.

6 Open the oven door and quickly drape the breads over the pebbles. Lower the heat to 110°C (225°F), Gas Mark ¼, and cook for 10–15 minutes until the top of the breads are dry and the bases are golden.

7 Ease the breads off the pebbles and wrap in a clean tea towel to keep them soft. Serve warm or cold, filled with salad or torn into pieces, with soup.

To make with a breadmaker

1 Lift the tin out of the bread machine, fit the kneader blade then add the measured cold water. Spoon in the flour then add the salt and sugar. Make a slight dip in the centre of the flour and sprinkle in the yeast (see page 14).

2 Insert the tin into the bread machine. Shut the lid and set to dough or basic dough. Press start.

3 Continue as step 3, left.

Makes 4

Tip Suitable pebbles can be bought from large garden centres and should be thoroughly scrubbed before using. Alternatively, cook the breads on preheated baking sheets.

6 little breads

Pretzels

Traditionally served in Germany with tankards of beer, pretzels can be bought from market stalls in a variety of sizes from tiny snack-sized nibbles to the giant dinner plate-sized breads for tearing and sharing.

325 g (11 oz, 3 cups) strong
   white flour
75 g (3 oz, ⅔ cup) rye flour
2 teaspoons soft light brown
   sugar
1 teaspoon salt
1 teaspoon fast-action dried yeast
275 ml (9 fl oz, heaping 1 cup)
   water

TO FINISH:
3 teaspoons fine salt
1 teaspoon caster sugar, optional
3 tablespoons water
coarse sea salt

To make by hand

1 Put the flours into a large bowl, then stir in the sugar, salt and yeast. Gradually mix in enough warm water to make a soft dough.

2 Knead well on a lightly floured surface for 5 minutes until the dough is smooth and elastic. Put the dough back into the bowl, cover loosely with oiled clingfilm and leave in a warm place to rise for 1 hour or until doubled in size.

3 Tip the dough out on to a floured surface, knead well then divide into 16 pieces. Shape each piece into a thin rope of about 30 cm (12 inches). Bend the rope so the dough forms a wide arc then, holding the ends of the rope in separate hands, twist them together in the centre and press the ends on to the curve to give a knotted effect (see page 19).

4 Transfer to a greased baking sheet and cover loosely with oiled clingfilm. Leave in a warm place to rise for 30 minutes or until half as big again.

5 Remove the clingfilm and bake the pretzels in a preheated oven, 200°C (400°F), Gas Mark 6, for 10 minutes until they are browned and sound hollow when tapped with the fingertips. Warm together the fine salt, sugar, if using, and water in a small saucepan to make the glaze, stirring until the salt and sugar have completely dissolved. Brush over the pretzels then sprinkle over the coarse salt.

6 Transfer to a wire rack to cool.

To make with a breadmaker

1 Lift the tin out of the bread machine, fit the kneader blade then add the water and sugar. Spoon in the flours and salt. Make a slight dip in the centre of the flour and sprinkle in the yeast (see page 14).

2 Insert the tin into the bread machine. Shut the lid and set to dough or basic dough. Press start.

3 At the end of the programme, lift the tin out of the machine, tip the dough out on to a lightly floured surface and continue as step 3, left.

Makes 16

> **Tip** Pretzels can also be cooked in boiling water, giving them a chewy texture (see page 22).

Sunburst rolls

475 g (15 oz, 4⅓ cups) strong
   white flour
2 tablespoons butter
1 teaspoon salt
1 teaspoon caster sugar
1¼ teaspoons fast-action dried
   yeast
275 ml (9 fl oz, heaping 1 cup)
   water
1 egg yolk, to glaze
1 tablespoon sesame seeds
2 teaspoons poppy seeds

To make by hand

1 Put the flour into a large bowl, add the butter and rub in with the fingertips until the mixture resembles fine breadcrumbs. Stir in the salt, sugar and yeast then gradually mix in enough warm water to make a soft dough.

2 Knead well on a lightly floured surface for 5 minutes until the dough is smooth and elastic. Put the dough back into the bowl, cover loosely with oiled clingfilm and leave in a warm place to rise for 1 hour or until doubled in size.

3 Tip the dough out on to a floured surface, knead well then cut into 16 pieces and shape each one into a ball. Arrange the dough balls in 2 rings inside a buttered deep-sided 25 cm (10 inch) round tin putting 10 rolls in the outer ring, 5 in the second ring and the last remaining roll in the centre.

4 Cover loosely with oiled clingfilm and leave in a warm place for 30 minutes until the rolls are well risen and touching.

5 Remove the clingfilm, brush with the egg yolk mixed with 1 tablespoon of water and sprinkle the outer ring and central roll with sesame seeds and the second ring with poppy seeds. Bake in a preheated oven, 200°C (400°F), Gas Mark 6, for 20–25 minutes until well risen and golden and the bread sounds hollow when tapped with the fingertips. Check after 15 minutes and cover with foil if overbrowning.

6 Holding the tin with oven gloves, loosen the edges of the rolls with a palette knife then turn them out on to a wire rack or large plate, then turn again on to a wire rack so that the tops of the rolls are uppermost. Leave to cool completely.

To make with a breadmaker

1 Lift the tin out of the bread machine, fit the kneader blade then add the measured cold water and butter. Spoon in the flour, then add the salt and sugar. Make a slight dip in the centre of the flour and sprinkle in the yeast (see page 15).

2 Insert the tin into the bread machine. Shut the lid and set to dough or basic dough. Press start.

3 At the end of the programme, lift the tin out of the bread machine and tip the dough on to a lightly floured surface and continue as step 3, left.

Makes 16

Tip If you find that the bread is a little soft after turning it out, return it to the oven, upturned on a baking sheet, for 5 minutes.

Fancy rolls

475 g (15 oz, 4⅓ cups) strong
white flour

2 tablespoons butter

1 teaspoon sugar

1 teaspoon salt

1¼ teaspoons fast-action dried
yeast

275 ml (9 fl oz, heaping 1 cup)
water

TO FINISH:

1 egg yolk, to glaze

poppy or black mustard seeds,
sesame seeds, fennel seeds,
paprika, sprigs of fresh
rosemary, coarsely ground
Cajun spice, coarse sea salt

To make by hand

1 Put the flour into a bowl, add the butter and rub in with the fingertips until the mixture resembles fine breadcrumbs. Stir in the sugar, salt and yeast then gradually mix in enough warm water to make a soft dough.

2 Knead well on a lightly floured surface for 5 minutes until the dough is smooth and elastic. Put the dough back into the bowl, cover loosely with oiled clingfilm and leave in a warm place to rise for 1 hour or until doubled in size.

3 Tip the dough out on to a lightly floured surface, knead well then cut into 12 pieces. Shape them as below then put on to greased baking sheets.

4 Cover loosely with oiled clingfilm and leave in a warm place to rise for 20 minutes.

5 Remove the clingfilm, brush with the egg yolk mixed with 1 tablespoon of water and sprinkle with seeds, spices, herbs or salt. Bake in a preheated oven, 200°C (400°F), Gas Mark 6, for 10 minutes until golden and the bases sound hollow when tapped with the fingertips. Transfer to a wire rack to cool.

To make with a breadmaker

1 Lift the tin out of the bread machine, fit the kneader blade then add the measured cold water and butter, cut into pieces. Spoon in the flour then add the sugar and salt. Make a slight dip in the centre of the flour and sprinkle in the yeast (see page 14).

2 Insert the tin into the bread machine. Shut the lid and set to dough or basic dough. Press start.

3 At the end of the programme, lift the tin out of the machine, tip the dough out on to a lightly floured surface, and continue as step 3, left.

Makes 12

Coils: take 2 pieces of dough and shape each one into a rope 25 cm (10 inches) long, roll up each rope along its length to make a spiral-like coil.

Clover leaf: take 2 pieces of dough and divide each one into 3 small balls, arrange in a triangle with the balls all touching each other.

Starburst: take 2 pieces of dough and shape each into a round. Make 5 or 6 cuts with scissors towards the centre of each one to resemble the spokes of a wheel.

Knots: take 2 pieces of dough and shape each one into a rope 22 cm (9 inches) long. Loop 1 end of 1 rope then thread the other end through the loop to make the knot. Repeat.

Herb split: take 2 pieces of dough and shape into an oval. Make 4 small cuts across the top of each with scissors and insert sprigs of rosemary into them. (Add fresh sprigs after baking too.)

Doughnuts

425 g (14 oz, 3¾ cups) strong
white flour

1 teaspoon salt

1 tablespoon caster sugar

2 tablespoons milk powder

1¼ teaspoons fast-action dried
yeast

2 eggs, beaten

175 ml (6 fl oz, ¾ cup) water

TO FINISH:

oil, for deep frying

75 g (3 oz, ⅓ cup) caster sugar

¾ teaspoon ground cinnamon

To make by hand

1 Mix the flour, salt, sugar, milk powder and yeast in a large bowl. Add the beaten eggs then gradually mix in enough warm water to make a soft dough.

2 Knead well on a lightly floured surface for 5 minutes until the dough is smooth and elastic. Put the dough back into the bowl, cover loosely with oiled clingfilm and leave in a warm place to rise for 1 hour or until doubled in size.

3 Tip out on to a lightly floured surface and knead well for 5 minutes. Roll out the dough to a thickness of 1 cm (½ inch) then stamp out circles using a 7 cm (3 inch) plain biscuit cutter. Use a finger to make a whole in the centre (see page 21). Carefully lift the doughnuts on to greased baking sheets, leaving plenty of space between them for rising.

4 Knead the dough trimmings together and continue rolling and cutting until all the dough is used up. Cover the doughnuts loosely with oiled clingfilm and leave to rise for 30 minutes or until half as big again.

5 Half fill a large saucepan with oil then heat to 180°C (350°F) or until a cube of bread sizzles the moment it is dropped into the oil. Carefully add the doughnuts to the hot oil one at a time, until there are three in the pan. Cook for 1–2 minutes until just beginning to brown, then turn over and cook until both sides are golden (see page 22).

6 Carefully lift the doughnuts out of the oil with a slotted spoon and place on a plate lined with kitchen paper. Continue frying the doughnuts until they are all cooked.

7 Transfer to a serving plate. Mix the sugar and cinnamon and sprinkle over the doughnuts.

To make with a breadmaker

1 Lift the tin out of the bread machine, fit the kneader blade then add the eggs and measured cold water. Spoon in the flour then add the salt, sugar and milk powder. Make a slight dip in the centre of the flour and sprinkle in the yeast (see page 14).

2 Insert the tin into the bread machine. Shut the lid and set to dough or basic dough. Press start.

3 At the end of the programme, lift the tin out of the machine, tip the dough out on to a lightly floured surface and continue as step 3, left.

Makes 12

Tip As these doughnuts contain fresh eggs, do not use the delay timer facility.

Crumpets

300 ml (½ pint, 1¼ cups) milk

300 ml (½ pint, 1¼ cups) water

425 g (14 oz, 3¾ cups) strong
white flour

1½ teaspoons salt

2 teaspoons fast-action dried
yeast

To make by hand

1 Warm the milk and the measured water in a small saucepan. Put the flour into a large bowl then stir in the salt and yeast. Gradually stir in the milk mixture to make a smooth thick batter.

2 Cover the top of the bowl with a clean tea towel and leave in a warm place for 1 hour or until the batter is well risen and bubbling.

3 Brush the inside of four plain 8 cm (3½ inch) biscuit cutters or individual flan rings with a little oil. Drizzle a little oil over a folded piece of kitchen paper and rub over the surface of a griddle or heavy-based nonstick frying pan, then heat.

4 Arrange the rings on the griddle or in the frying pan then, using a large serving spoon, spoon enough batter into the moulds to make a depth of about 1 cm (½ inch). Cook gently (see page 22) until the batter has bubbled and looks dry on the surface. Loosen the rings and remove, then turn over the crumpets and cook the other side until pale golden.

5 To keep them warm, wrap the cooked crumpets in a clean tea towel set on a plate. Cook a second batch of crumpets in the same way and continue cooking and refilling the rings, greasing the tins and the griddle or pan with oil as needed, until all the batter is used up.

6 Reheat the crumpets under the grill, cooking the top side only. Spread with butter and jam or honey.

To make with a breadmaker

1 Lift the tin out of the bread machine, fit the kneader blade then add the milk and measured cold water. Spoon in the flour then add the salt. Make a slight dip in the centre of the flour and sprinkle in the yeast (see page 14).

2 Insert the tin into the bread machine. Shut the lid and set to dough or basic dough. Press start. Do not use the delay timer facility.

3 Stop the machine after 1 hour. At this stage you should have a thick bubbling dough that is just a little thicker than a batter mixture. Continue as step 3, left.

Makes 18

> **Tips** If you don't have four biscuit cutters the same size, then improvise with four shallow cans with the tops and bottoms removed. Wash them well in hot soapy water and remove the labels.
>
> Use a large plastic spoon to spoon the batter out of the bread machine so that you don't scratch the nonstick lining.

Mini barley flower pot loaves

Bread has been traditionally made in flower pots for many years, but it is notoriously difficult to turn the bread out of them. These mini loaves, flavoured with barley malt extract and barley flakes, are shaped in individual metal dessert moulds, so they look just the same, but are much easier (and more hygienic) to use.

400 g (13 oz, 3⅔ cups) strong
   coarse brown flour
2 tablespoons butter
1 teaspoon salt
1 teaspoon caster sugar
2 tablespoons milk powder
50 g (2 oz, ¼ cup) barley flakes
1¼ teaspoons fast-action dried
   yeast
2 tablespoons barley malt extract
275 ml (9 fl oz, 1 cup plus
   2 tablespoons) water
2 tablespoons milk, to glaze
extra barley flakes

To make by hand

1 Put the flour into a large bowl, add the butter and rub in with the fingertips until the mixture resembles fine breadcrumbs. Stir in the salt, sugar, milk powder, barley flakes and yeast. Add the malt extract and enough warm water to make a soft dough.

2 Knead well on a lightly floured surface for 5 minutes until the dough is smooth and elastic. Put it back into the bowl, cover loosely with oiled clingfilm and leave in a warm place for 1 hour or until doubled in size.

3 Tip the dough out on to a lightly floured surface and knead well. Cut into 10 pieces and shape each into a ball. Press into 10 greased 150 ml (¼ pint) individual plain dessert moulds or large dariole tins.

4 Transfer the moulds to a baking sheet. Cover loosely with oiled clingfilm and leave in a warm place to rise for 30 minutes or until the dough reaches just above the top of the tins.

5 Remove the clingfilm, brush the tops with milk and sprinkle with a few extra barley flakes. Bake in a preheated oven, 200°C (400°F), Gas Mark 6, for 12–15 minutes until the breads are well risen, browned and sound hollow when tapped with the fingertips.

6 Holding the tins with oven gloves, loosen the edges of the breads with a small palette knife. Transfer to a wire rack to cool.

To make with a breadmaker

1 Lift the tin out of the bread machine, fit the kneader blade then add the measured cold water, milk powder, butter and malt extract. Spoon in the flour and barley flakes then add the salt and sugar. Make a slight dip in the centre of the flour and sprinkle in the yeast (see page 14).

2 Insert the tin into the bread machine. Shut the lid and set to dough or basic dough. Press start.

3 At the end of the programme, lift the tin out of the machine, tip the dough out on to a lightly floured surface and continue as step 3, left.

Makes 10

Tip Barley malt extract is available from health food shops.

Bagels

500 g (1 lb, 4½ cups) strong
   white flour
2 tablespoons caster sugar
1 teaspoon salt
1¼ teaspoons fast-action dried
   yeast
300 ml (½ pint, 1¼ cups) water
1 egg yolk, to glaze
3 tablespoons poppy or sesame
   seeds

To make by hand

1 Put the flour, 1 tablespoon of the sugar, salt and yeast into a large bowl. Gradually mix in enough warm water to make a soft dough.

2 Knead on a lightly floured surface for 5 minutes until the dough is smooth and elastic then put back into the bowl. Cover loosely with oiled clingfilm and leave in a warm place for 1 hour or until doubled in size.

3 Tip the dough out on to a lightly floured surface, knead well then cut into 10 equal pieces. Shape each into a ball then make a hole about 3.5 cm (1½ inches) in the centre of each one with a well-floured finger (see page 21). Enlarge the hole by adding a second finger and moving your fingers round and round.

4 Transfer the bagels to 2 baking sheets lined with nonstick baking paper. Cover loosely with oiled clingfilm and leave in a warm place to rise for 30 minutes or until half as big again.

5 When the bagels are nearly ready, pour 2 litres (3½ pints, 8 cups) of water into a large saucepan, add the remaining sugar and bring to the boil.

6 Carefully lower the bagels one at a time into the boiling water for 1–2 minutes each side or until they float (see page 22). Lift the bagels out of the water with a slotted spoon and put them back on the baking sheets to drain.

7 Transfer to 2 greased baking sheets. Brush with egg yolk mixed with 1 tablespoon of water and sprinkle with seeds. Bake in a preheated oven, 200°C (400°F), Gas Mark 6, for 12–15 minutes until they are golden brown and sound hollow when tapped with the fingertips. Transfer to a wire rack to cool.

To make with a breadmaker

1 Lift the tin out of the bread machine, fit the kneader blade then add the measured cold water. Spoon in the flour then add 1 tablespoon of the sugar and the salt. Make a slight dip in the centre of the flour and sprinkle in the yeast (see page 14).

2 Insert the tin into the bread machine. Shut the lid and set to dough or basic dough. Press start.

3 At the end of the programme, lift the tin out of the machine, tip the dough out on to a lightly floured surface and continue as step 3, left.

Makes 10

Tip If liked add ground cinnamon or fresh blueberries and a little sugar to the bagel dough. For a savoury version, add some thinly sliced fried onions.

Brioche

250 g (8 oz, 2¼ cups) strong
   white flour
½ teaspoon salt
2 tablespoons caster sugar
1 teaspoon fast-action dried yeast
75 g (3 oz, ¼ cup plus 2
   tablespoons) butter, softened
3 eggs, beaten
1 egg yolk, to glaze

These buttery, lightly sweetened French rolls are baked in mini fluted tins for their characteristic shape.

To make by hand

1 Put the flour, salt, sugar and yeast into a large bowl. Melt 2 tablespoons of the butter then stir it into the bowl with the beaten eggs. Mix to a soft dough.

2 Knead well on a lightly floured surface for 5 minutes until the dough is smooth and elastic. Put the dough back into the bowl, cover loosely with oiled clingfilm and leave in a warm place to rise for 1¼–1½ hours or until doubled in size.

3 Tip the dough out on to a lightly floured surface and knead well. Brush 10 brioche tins, 8 cm (3½ inch), with a little of the butter, then cut the remaining butter into small pieces and gradually knead it into the dough. The dough will appear quite greasy at first, but don't be tempted to keep sprinkling the work surface with more flour – the more you knead, the smoother the dough will become.

4 Cut off 10 tiny pieces of dough (about the size of your fingernail) and reserve for the tops. Cut the rest of the dough into 10 larger pieces. Shape each one into a smooth ball and transfer to the tins.

5 Shape the tiny pieces of dough into balls, place on the larger ones and press the handle of a teaspoon down through the little ball to the one beneath. Put the tins on to a baking sheet, cover loosely with oiled clingfilm and leave in a warm place for 30 minutes or until the dough reaches the top of the tins.

6 Remove the clingfilm and brush with the egg yolk mixed with 1 tablespoon of water. Bake in a preheated oven, 200°C (400°F), Gas Mark 6, for 10 minutes until golden. Loosen the edges of the brioche and transfer to a wire rack to cool.

To make with a breadmaker

1 Lift the tin out of the bread machine, fit the kneader blade then add 2 tablespoons of the butter and the beaten eggs. Spoon in the flour then add the salt and sugar. Make a slight dip in the centre of the flour and add the yeast (see page 14).

2 Insert the tin into the bread machine. Shut the lid and set to dough or enriched dough setting. Press start.

3 Continue as step 3, left.

Makes 10

> **Tip** As these rolls contain fresh eggs and butter, do not use the delay timer facility.

Drizzled orange and poppy seed buns

500 g (1 lb, 4½ cups) strong
white flour

2 tablespoons butter

2 tablespoons milk powder

1 teaspoon salt

40 g (1½ oz, 3 tablespoons)
poppy seeds

1 orange, grated rind and juice

1¼ teaspoons fast-action dried
yeast

4 tablespoons (¼ cup) honey

275 ml (9 fl oz, heaping 1 cup)
water

1 egg yolk

200 g (7 oz, 1¾ cups) icing sugar

To make by hand

1 Put the flour into a large bowl, add the butter and rub in with the fingertips until the mixture resembles fine breadcrumbs. Stir in the milk powder, salt, poppy seeds, grated orange rind and yeast. Add the honey then gradually mix in enough warm water to make a soft dough.

2 Knead well on a lightly floured surface for 5 minutes until the dough is smooth and elastic. Put the dough back into the bowl, cover loosely with oiled clingfilm and leave in a warm place to rise for 1 hour or until doubled in size.

3 Tip the dough out on to a lightly floured surface, knead well then cut into 20 pieces. Shape each piece into a small ball and arrange, spaced well apart, on a greased baking sheet.

4 Cover loosely with oiled clingfilm and leave to rise for 30 minutes or until half as big again.

5 Remove the clingfilm, brush with the egg yolk mixed with 1 tablespoon of water and bake in a preheated oven, 200°C (400°F), Gas Mark 6, for 12–15 minutes until the buns are golden and sound hollow when tapped with the fingertips. Transfer to a wire rack and leave to cool for 15 minutes.

6 Sift the icing sugar into a bowl then gradually mix in the juice of half the orange or enough to make a smooth spoonable icing. Drizzle the icing over the buns with a spoon making random zigzag lines. Leave for at least 15 minutes so that the icing can harden.

To make with a breadmaker

1 Lift the tin out of the bread machine, fit the kneader blade then add the measured cold water, milk powder, butter, honey, poppy seeds and orange rind. Spoon in the flour then add the salt. Make a dip in the centre of the flour and sprinkle in the yeast (see page 14).

2 Insert the tin into the bread machine. Shut the lid and set to dough or basic dough. Press start.

3 At the end of the programme, lift the tin out of the machine, tip the dough out on to a lightly floured surface and continue as step 3, left.

Makes 20

Tip Instead of the poppy seeds, try adding 125 g (4 oz, ½ cup) roughly chopped glacé cherries either when the raisin beep sounds or, if making by hand, when kneading the dough for the first time.

Croissants

400 g (13 oz, 3⅔ cups) strong
white flour

½ teaspoon salt

1 tablespoon caster sugar

2 teaspoons fast-action dried
yeast

150 g (5 oz, ½ cup plus 2
tablespoons) butter, softened

1 egg, beaten

175 ml (6 fl oz, ¾ cup) water

1 egg yolk, to glaze

To make by hand

1 Put the flour into a large bowl. Stir in the salt, sugar and yeast. Rub in 25 g (1 oz, 2 tablespoons) of the butter with the fingertips until the mixture resembles fine breadcrumbs. Add the beaten egg then mix in enough warm water to make a soft dough.

2 Knead the dough for 5 minutes until smooth and elastic. Return to the bowl, cover with oiled clingfilm and leave in a warm place until doubled in size.

3 Meanwhile, roll the remaining butter between 2 sheets of greaseproof paper to a rectangle 30 x 7 cm (12 x 3 inches). Freeze for 10 minutes.

4 Tip the dough out on to a lightly floured surface, knead well and roll out to a rectangle about 2.5 cm (1 inch) larger than the butter all the way round.

5 Peel the paper off the butter and place the butter on top of the dough. Fold the bottom third of the dough over, then fold the top third up and over the bottom third (see page 18). Give the bread parcel a quarter turn and repeat the rolling and folding.

6 Wrap the dough in greaseproof paper and chill for 10 minutes. Repeat the rolling and folding twice, turning between each folding. Chill for 20 minutes, roll and fold twice more. Chill again for 20 minutes.

7 Roll the dough out to a 25 x 37 cm (10 x 15 inch) rectangle. Cut into 6 squares then cut each square into two triangles. Roll up the triangles (see page 19) and put on a greased baking sheet. Cover with oiled clingfilm and leave in a warm place for 45 minutes.

8 Remove clingfilm and brush with egg yolk mixed with 1 tablespoon water. Bake in a preheated oven, 180°C (350°F), Gas Mark 4, for 10 minutes until golden.

To make with a breadmaker

1 Lift the tin out of the bread machine, fit the kneader blade then add the measured cold water, 25 g (1 oz, 2 tablespoons) of the butter, cut into pieces, and the beaten egg. Spoon in the flour then add the salt and sugar. Make a slight dip in the centre of the flour and sprinkle in the yeast (see page 14).

2 Insert the tin into the bread machine. Shut the lid and set to dough or basic dough. Press start.

3 Continue as step 3, left.

Makes 12

Tip If the dough becomes very sticky when rolling and folding, simply wrap it in greaseproof paper and chill in the refrigerator for 10–20 minutes and then try again. The more you roll and fold the dough, the more flaky the finished croissants will be.

Danish pastries

500 g (1 lb, 4½ cups) strong
   white flour
2 tablespoons caster sugar
2 teaspoons fast-action dried
   yeast
1 egg, beaten
275 ml (9 fl oz, 1 cup plus
   2 tablespoons) milk
200 g (7 oz, ¾ cup plus
   2 tablespoons) unsalted butter,
   softened

FOR THE FILLING:
75 g (3 oz, ¼ cup plus 2
   tablespoons) unsalted butter,
   softened
75 g (3 oz, ⅓ cup) caster sugar
75 g (3 oz, ⅓ cup plus
   2 tablespoons) ground almonds
few drops almond essence
16 apricot halves
1 beaten egg, to glaze
425 g (14 oz) can apricot halves,
   drained

TO FINISH:
2 tablespoons apricot jam

To make by hand

1 Put the flour, sugar and yeast into a large bowl. Add the beaten egg then gradually mix in enough warm milk to make a soft dough.

2 Knead well on a floured surface for 5 minutes until the dough is smooth and elastic. Put back into the bowl, cover with oiled clingfilm and leave in a warm place to rise for 1 hour or until doubled in size.

3 About 20 minutes before the end of the rising time, put the butter between 2 large pieces of greaseproof paper and roll out to a 37 x 18 cm (15 x 7 inch) rectangle. Freeze for 10 minutes.

4 Tip the dough out on to a lightly floured surface and knead well. Take the butter out of the freezer and roll out the dough to a rectangle about 2.5 cm (1 inch) larger than the butter all the way round.

5 Peel the paper off the butter and put on to the dough. Fold the bottom third of the dough over, then fold the top third up and over the bottom third (see page 18). Give the bread parcel a quarter turn and repeat the rolling and folding.

6 Wrap the dough in clean greaseproof paper and chill for 10 minutes. Repeat the rolling and folding process twice more, giving the dough a quarter turn between each folding and rolling.

7 Chill the dough for 20 minutes. To make the filling, beat the butter and sugar together until light and fluffy then gradually beat in the ground almonds and almond essence.

8 Roll the dough out thinly and trim to a 40 cm (16 inch) square, then cut into smaller 10 cm (4 inch) squares. Dot the almond filling over the centre of the squares, then brush the edges with beaten egg. Lift the 2 opposite corners of the squares up and over the almond filling and press the ends together. Top with an apricot half. Transfer to 2 baking sheets and brush with the beaten egg.

9 Loosely cover the pastries with oiled clingfilm and leave to rise in a warm place for 30 minutes or until half as big again.

10 Bake in a preheated oven, 200°C (400°F), Gas Mark 6, for 8 minutes, reduce the temperature to 180°C (350°F), Gas Mark 4, for a further 5–7 minutes until the pastries are golden brown. Brush the apricot halves with warmed jam then transfer to a wire rack to cool.

To make with a breadmaker

1 Lift the tin out of the bread machine, fit the kneader blade then add the milk and beaten egg. Spoon in the flour then add the sugar. Make a dip in the centre of the flour and sprinkle in the yeast (see page 14).

2 Insert the tin into the bread machine. Shut the lid and set to dough or basic dough. Press start.

3 Continue as step 3, left.

Makes 16

> **Tips** If the dough becomes very sticky when rolling and folding, wrap it in greaseproof paper, chill in the refrigerator for 10–20 minutes and then try again.
> As these pastries contain fresh milk and an egg, do not use the delay timer facility.

Surprise chocolate mini loaves

250 g (8 oz, 2¼ cups) strong
   white flour

2 tablespoons butter

½ teaspoon salt

2 tablespoons sugar

¾ teaspoon fast-action dried yeast

2 eggs, beaten

3 tablespoons milk

50 g (2 oz) plain dark chocolate

TO DECORATE:

cocoa powder

icing sugar

To make by hand

1 Put the flour into a large bowl. Stir in the salt, sugar and yeast then rub in the butter with the fingertips until the mixture resembles fine breadcrumbs. Add the beaten eggs and enough warm milk to make a soft dough.

2 Knead well on a lightly floured surface for 5 minutes until the dough is smooth and elastic. Put the dough back into the bowl, cover loosely with oiled clingfilm and leave in a warm place to rise for 1 hour or until doubled in size.

3 Tip out the dough on to a lightly floured surface, knead well then cut into 6 pieces. Cut the chocolate into 6 pieces. Roll 1 piece of dough at a time to a rectangle 7 x 10 cm (3 x 4 inches), add 1 piece of the chocolate then wrap the dough around it and transfer to a greased 10 x 5.5 x 3.5 cm (4 x 2¼ x 1½ inch) mini loaf tin. Repeat to fill 6 tins.

4 Put the loaf tins on to a baking sheet, cover the tops loosely with oiled clingfilm and leave in a warm place for 40 minutes until they are well risen and the dough reaches just above the tops of the tins.

5 Remove the clingfilm, bake in a preheated oven, 200°C (400°F), Gas Mark 6, for 12–15 minutes until the breads are well risen and golden and sound hollow when tapped with the fingertips.

6 Holding the tins with oven gloves, loosen the edges of the breads with a small palette knife. Transfer to a wire rack to cool. Decorate with a little sifted cocoa and icing sugar.

To make with a breadmaker

1 Lift the tin out of the bread machine, fit the kneader blade then add the butter, beaten eggs and milk. Spoon in the flour then add the salt and sugar. Make a slight dip in the centre of the flour and add the yeast (see page 14).

2 Insert the tin into the bread machine. Shut the lid and set to dough or basic dough. Press start.

3 At the end of the programme, lift the tin out of the machine, tip the dough out on to a lightly floured surface and continue as step 3, left.

Makes 6

> **Tip** If you don't have mini loaf tins then shape the dough into rolls instead.

festive breads

Fougasse

Traditionally made in Provence in southern France to celebrate Reveillon or Christmas Eve, this flat bread is eaten as part of a mixed feast with 12 other dishes, both sweet and savoury, to symbolize Christ and his disciples. The cuts in the loaves are meant to suggest the branches of a tree.

475 g (15 oz, 4⅓ cups) strong white flour

1½ teaspoons salt

2 teaspoons caster sugar

3 tablespoons fresh chopped or 1½ teaspoons dried mixed herbs such as lavender, thyme, and rosemary

1¼ teaspoons fast-action dried yeast

4 tablespoons (¼ cup) olive oil

250 ml (8 fl oz, 1 cup) water

TO FINISH:

extra olive oil

coarse sea salt

To make by hand

1 Put the flour into a large bowl then stir in the salt, sugar, herbs and yeast. Add the oil then gradually mix in enough warm water to make a soft dough.

2 Knead well on a lightly floured surface for 5 minutes until the dough is smooth and elastic. Put the dough back into the bowl, cover loosely with oiled clingfilm and leave in a warm place to rise for 1 hour or until doubled in size.

3 Tip the dough out on to a lightly floured surface, knead well then cut in half. Roll each half out to an oval of about 30 x 20 cm (12 x 8 inches).

4 Transfer to 2 greased baking sheets. Make 5 diagonal slits in the bread then open out the outer edges of the slits by lifting the edges of the bread and widening the gap with a fingertip (see page 21).

5 Cover loosely with oiled clingfilm and leave in a warm place to rise for 30 minutes or until puffy.

6 Remove the clingfilm and bake in a preheated oven, 220°C (425°F), Gas Mark 7, for 8–10 minutes until golden. Drizzle with a little olive oil and scatter over a little sea salt. Transfer to a wire rack after 10 minutes and leave to cool completely.

To make with a breadmaker

1 Lift the tin out of the bread machine, fit the kneader blade then add the measured cold water and olive oil. Spoon in the flour then add the salt, sugar and herbs. Make a slight dip in the centre of the flour and sprinkle in the yeast (see page 14).

2 Insert the tin into the bread machine. Shut the lid and set to dough or basic dough. Press start.

3 At the end of the programme, lift the tin out of the machine, tip the dough out on to a lightly floured surface and continue as step 3, left.

Makes 2 large flat breads

Tip Chopped black olives, fried onion slices or fennel seeds also make good additions.

Panetonne

This Italian speciality is always served at Christmas, often as a celebratory snack after returning home from midnight mass on Christmas Eve.

400 g (13 oz, 3¾ cups) strong white flour

75 g (3 oz, ⅓ cup) butter, at room temperature, cubed

50 g (2 oz, ¼ cup) caster sugar

a pinch of nutmeg

1 lemon, finely grated rind only

½ orange, finely grated rind only

1¾ teaspoons fast-action dried yeast

2 eggs, beaten

150 ml (¼ pint, ⅔ cup) milk

125 g (4 oz, ½ cup) mixed dried fruit

50 g (2 oz, ¼ cup) diced candied peel

TO DECORATE:

icing sugar

To make by hand

1 Put the flour into a large bowl, add the butter and rub in with the fingertips until the mixture resembles fine breadcrumbs. Stir in the sugar, nutmeg, fruit rinds and yeast. Add the beaten eggs then gradually mix in enough warm milk to make a soft dough.

2 Knead well on a lightly floured surface for 5 minutes until smooth and elastic. Gradually work in the fruit and candied peel then put the dough back into the bowl. Cover with oiled clingfilm and leave in a warm place to rise for 1¼ hours or until doubled in size.

3 Meanwhile, line the sides of a deep 18 cm (7 inch) round cake tin with a double thickness of nonstick baking paper 15 cm (6 inches) deep and the base with a single circle of nonstick baking paper.

4 Tip the dough out on to a lightly floured surface and knead well. Press into the tin then cover loosely with oiled clingfilm or nonstick baking paper and leave in a warm place for 45 minutes or until the dough reaches just above the top of the tin.

5 Bake in a preheated oven, 180°C (350°F), Gas Mark 4, for 45 minutes until the bread is a deep golden brown and sounds hollow when tapped with the fingertips. Check after 20 minutes and cover with foil if overbrowning.

6 Holding the tin with oven gloves, loosen the gap between the lining paper and tin with a palette knife then invert the bread on to a wire rack. Quickly peel off the paper, turn the bread up the right way and leave to cool. Dust liberally with sifted icing sugar.

To make with a breadmaker

1 Lift the tin out of the bread machine, fit the kneader blade then add the milk, eggs, butter, sugar, nutmeg and fruit rinds. Spoon in the flour. Make a slight dip in the centre of the flour and sprinkle in the yeast (see page 14).

2 Insert the tin into the bread machine. Shut the lid and set to dough or enriched dough. Press start.

3 When the raisin beep sounds, add the mixed dried fruit and candied peel, shut the lid and allow the programme to continue.

4 Continue as step 3, left.

Makes 1 large loaf

> **Tip** For a real Christmas touch, cut a star shape out of nonstick baking paper, place it on top of the bread then dust with icing sugar and remove the paper.

Three kings ring

This rich, sweet bread ring is made in Spanish-speaking countries to mark Epiphany.

500 g (1 lb, 4½ cups) strong
   white flour

1 teaspoon salt

1 orange, grated rind only

1 lemon, grated rind only

125 g (4 oz, ½ cup) caster sugar

1½ teaspoons fast-action dried
   yeast

75 g (3 oz, ⅓ cup) butter, melted

2 eggs, beaten

175 ml (6 fl oz, ¾ cup) water

100 g (3½ oz, ½ cup) whole
   candied peel

125 g (4 oz, ½ cup) glacé
   cherries

125 g (4 oz, 1½ cups) blanched
   almonds, cut into slivers

TO FINISH:

125 g (4 oz, 1 cup plus
   2 tablespoons) icing sugar

4–5 teaspoons orange or lemon
   juice

To make by hand

1 Put the flour in a large bowl then stir in the salt, grated fruit rinds, sugar and yeast. Add the melted butter and beaten eggs then gradually mix in enough warm water to make a soft dough.

2 Knead well on a lightly floured surface until the dough is smooth and elastic. Put back into the bowl and cover with oiled clingfilm. Leave in a warm place to rise for 1¼ hours or until doubled in size.

3 Tip the dough out on to a lightly floured surface and knead well. Roughly chop the candied peel, cherries and almonds. Reserve one-third of the mixture then gradually knead the remainder into the dough.

4 Shape the dough into a thick rope 50 cm (20 inches) long and squeeze together the ends to make a ring. Place on to a greased baking sheet. Wrap the pea and other tiny presents in foil and press into the underside of the dough. Stand a greased, heatproof bowl in the centre of the ring to keep the hole shape and cover loosely with oiled clingfilm. Leave to rise for 30 minutes or until half as big again.

5 Remove the clingfilm and bowl. Brush with the egg yolk mixed with 1 tablespoon of water. Bake in a preheated oven, 200°C (400°F), Gas Mark 6, for 20–25 minutes until the bread is golden brown and sounds hollow when tapped with the fingertips. Cover with foil if overbrowning.

6 Transfer to a wire rack to cool. Sift the icing sugar into a bowl then gradually mix in the orange or lemon juice to make a smooth, pouring icing. Drizzle over the bread in random lines. Sprinkle with the reserved fruit and nuts then leave to set.

To make with a breadmaker

1 Lift the tin out of the bread machine, fit the kneader blade then add the measured cold water, beaten eggs, melted butter and sugar. Spoon in the flour then add the salt and grated fruit rinds. Make a slight dip in the centre of the flour and sprinkle in the yeast (see page 14).

2 Insert the tin into the bread machine, shut the lid and set to dough or enriched dough. Press start.

3 At the end of the programme, lift the tin out of the machine, tip the dough out on to a lightly floured surface and continue as step 3, left.

Makes 1 large loaf

Tips Traditionally, this bread contains a dried pea and two other tiny foil-wrapped gifts – if you do add any gifts, make sure they are heatproof.

As this bread contains fresh eggs and butter, do not use the delay timer facility.

Warm milk may be used instead of water, if liked.

Stollen

This famous, sweet German Christmas bread is delicately perfumed with spices and lemon rind then wrapped around a rich marzipan filling and shaped to resemble the baby Jesus wrapped in swaddling clothes.

125 g (4 oz, ½ cup) mixed dried
   fruit and candied peel
3 tablespoons rum
500 g (1 lb, 4½ cups) strong
   white flour
½ teaspoon salt
125 g (4 oz, ½ cup) caster sugar
½ teaspoon ground nutmeg
¼ teaspoon ground cardamom
1 small lemon, grated rind only
1½ teaspoons fast-action dried
   yeast
175 g (6 oz, ¾ cup) butter
1 egg, beaten
175 ml (6 fl oz, ¾ cup) milk

FOR THE MARZIPAN:
125 g (4 oz, ½ cup/1 stick) butter
125 g (4 oz, ½ cup) caster sugar
125 g (4 oz, ¾ cup) ground
   almonds
¼ teaspoon almond essence
2 tablespoons plain flour
1 egg, beaten

TO FINISH:
25 g (1 oz, 2 tablespoons) butter,
   melted
25 g (1 oz, ¼ cup) icing sugar

To make by hand

1 Begin as step 1, right.

2 Put the flour into a large bowl, then stir in the salt, sugar, spices, lemon rind and yeast. Add 50 g (2 oz, ¼ cup) melted butter and the beaten egg then gradually mix in enough milk to make a soft dough.

3 Knead for 5 minutes until smooth and elastic. Return to bowl, cover with oiled clingfilm and leave to rise in a warm place for 1¼ hours or until doubled in size.

4 Meanwhile, to make the marzipan, beat 125 g (4 oz, ½ cup/1 stick) butter and sugar together until light and fluffy. Add the almonds, almond essence, flour and beaten egg and mix together. Shape into a rope about 37 cm (15 inches) long. Chill until required.

5 Knead the dough well. Cut the remaining butter into pieces and knead a few pieces at a time into the dough. Alternate with spoonfuls of dried fruit.

6 Wrap the dough in greaseproof paper and chill for 20 minutes. Roll out on a lightly floured surface to an oval of about 15 x 40 cm (6 x 16 inches). Lay the marzipan in the centre and wrap the dough around.

7 Transfer to a greased baking sheet. Cover with oiled clingfilm and leave to rise for 30 minutes.

8 Remove the clingfilm. Bake in a preheated oven, 180°C (350°F), Gas Mark 4, for 25–30 minutes until the bread is golden and sounds hollow when tapped.

9 Transfer to a wire rack. Brush with the remaining melted butter and sprinkle with sifted icing sugar.

To make with a breadmaker

1 Put the dried fruits and candied peel into a bowl, pour over the rum then cover the bowl with a saucer and leave overnight to soak.

2 Melt 50 g (2 oz, ¼ cup) of the butter. Lift the tin out of the bread machine, fit the kneader blade then add the melted butter, beaten egg and milk. Spoon in the flour, salt, sugar, spices and lemon rind. Make a slight dip in the centre of the flour and sprinkle in the yeast (see page 14).

3 Insert the tin into the bread machine. Shut the lid and set to dough or enriched dough. Press start.

4 Continue as step 4, left.

Makes 1 loaf

Tips Homemade marzipan can be replaced with 375 g (12 oz, 1½ cups) of shop-bought marzipan.
   As this bread contains fresh butter and an egg, do not use the delay timer facility.
   If you are making the dough by hand and find that it is very sticky at Step 5, leave it on the work surface for 10 minutes to absorb the butter. Try to resist the urge to keep flouring the work surface.

Pulla

Originally from Finland, this butter and egg-enriched dough is delicately flavoured with saffron and ground cardamom. It is delicious served with unsalted butter and apricot jam.

large pinch of saffron threads

275 ml (9 fl oz, heaping 1 cup) hand-hot water

12 cardamom pods

475 g (15 oz, 4⅓ cups) strong white flour

3 tablespoons butter

¼ teaspoon salt

1½ teaspoons fast-action dried yeast

4 tablespoons (¼ cup) honey

1 egg, beaten

egg yolk, to glaze

50 g (2 oz, ¼ cup) piece orange citron peel, cut into thin strips

To make by hand

1 Infuse the saffron for 10 minutes only and crush the cardamom as step 1, right.

2 Put the flour into a large bowl, add the butter and rub in with the fingertips until the mixture resembles fine breadcrumbs. Stir in the salt, ground cardamom and yeast then add the honey and beaten egg. Warm the saffron and the soaking water then gradually stir in to the mixture to make a smooth, soft dough.

3 Knead well on a lightly floured surface for 5 minutes until the dough is smooth and elastic. Put the dough back into the bowl, cover loosely with oiled clingfilm and leave in a warm place to rise for 1 hour or until doubled in size.

4 Tip the dough out on to a lightly floured surface, knead well then cut into 3 pieces. Shape each piece into a rope about 37 cm (15 inches) long. Plait the ropes together (see page 20).

5 Lift the plait on to a large greased baking sheet and shape into a round, tucking the ends of the rope underneath so that the plait looks continuous (see page 20). Cover loosely with oiled clingfilm and leave in a warm place to rise for 40 minutes.

6 Remove the clingfilm. Brush the ring with the egg yolk mixed with 1 tablespoon of water, sprinkle with orange strips and bake in a preheated oven, 200°C (400°F), Gas Mark 6, for 20 minutes until the bread is golden and sounds hollow when tapped with the fingertips. Check after 10 minutes and cover with foil if overbrowning. Transfer to a wire rack to cool.

To make with a breadmaker

1 Put the saffron into a bowl with the measured water and leave to infuse for 30 minutes or until cold. Peel the green pods off the cardamom and grind the black seeds using a pestle and mortar.

2 Lift the tin out of the bread machine, fit the kneader blade then add the saffron and the (now tepid) soaking water, ground cardamom, butter cut into pieces, beaten egg and honey. Spoon in the flour then add the salt. Make a dip in the centre of the flour and add the yeast (see page 14).

3 Insert the tin into the bread machine. Shut the lid and set to dough or enriched dough. Press start.

4 At the end of the programme, lift the tin out of the machine, tip the dough out on to a lightly floured surface and continue as step 4, left.

Makes 1 ring loaf

Hot cross buns

Versions of hot cross buns have been made since pagan times, originally cut into a cross to symbolize the four seasons, and later used as a sign to ward off evil spirits. These delicately spiced, sweet, fruity buns are now made and eaten on Good Friday to commemorate Jesus carrying the cross.

500 g (1 lb, 4½ cups) strong
   white flour
3 tablespoons butter
3 tablespoons caster sugar
1 teaspoon salt
1 teaspoon ground cinnamon
¼ teaspoon ground allspice
¼ teaspoon grated nutmeg
1½ teaspoons fast-action dried
   yeast
1 egg, beaten
275 ml (9 fl oz, 1 cup plus
   2 tablespoons) milk
125 g (4 oz, ½ cup) raisins

FOR THE CROSSES:
125 g (4 oz, 1⅛ cups) strong
   white or plain flour
8–9 tablespoons (½ cup) water

TO GLAZE:
4 tablespoons (¼ cup) milk
2 tablespoons caster sugar

To make by hand

1 Put the flour into a large bowl, add the butter and rub in with the fingertips until the mixture resembles fine breadcrumbs. Stir in the sugar, salt, spices and yeast. Add the beaten egg then gradually mix in enough milk to make a smooth soft dough.

2 Knead well on a lightly floured surface for 5 minutes until the dough is smooth and elastic. Gradually work in the raisins then put the dough back into the bowl. Cover loosely with oiled clingfilm and leave in a warm place to rise for 1 hour or until doubled in size.

3 Tip the dough out on to a lightly floured surface and knead well. Cut into 12 even pieces then, with lightly floured hands, shape each into a ball. Put the buns, spaced well apart, on to a greased baking sheet.

4 Cover loosely with oiled clingfilm and leave in a warm place to rise for 30 minutes.

5 Sift the flour for the crosses into a small bowl then gradually mix in the measured water to make a smooth paste. Spoon into a greaseproof paper piping bag and snip off the tip. Pipe crosses over the buns then quickly transfer to a preheated oven, 200°C (400°F), Gas Mark 6, and bake the buns for 15 minutes until golden brown.

6 Meanwhile, put the milk and sugar into a small saucepan, heat gently until the sugar has dissolved then boil for 2–3 minutes until it is syrupy. Brush the hot glaze over the buns (see page 23).

7 After 5 minutes transfer buns to a wire rack to cool.

To make with a breadmaker

1 Lift the tin out of the bread machine, fit the kneader blade then add the milk, beaten egg, sugar and butter. Spoon in the flour then add the salt and spices. Make a slight dip in the centre of the flour then sprinkle in the yeast (see page 14).

2 Insert the tin into the bread machine. Shut the lid and set to dough or enriched dough. Press start.

3 When the raisin beep sounds, add the raisins, shut the lid and allow the programme to continue.

4 At the end of the programme, lift the tin out of the machine, tip the dough out on to a lightly floured surface and continue as step 3, left.

Makes 12 buns

Tip As these buns contain fresh milk and an egg, do not use the delay timer facility.

Challah

This coiled, egg-enriched loaf is baked for the Jewish new year and symbolizes continuity because it has no beginning and no end.

500 g (1 lb, 4½ cups) strong white flour

1 teaspoon salt

1¼ teaspoons fast-action dried yeast

50 g (2 oz, ¼ cup) butter, melted

2 eggs, beaten

3 tablespoons clear honey

175 ml (6 fl oz, ¾ cup) water

1 egg yolk, to glaze

2 teaspoons poppy seeds

To make by hand

1 Put the flour, salt and yeast into a large bowl. Add the melted butter, beaten eggs and honey then gradually mix in enough warm water to make a soft dough.

2 Knead well on a lightly floured surface for 5 minutes until the dough is smooth and elastic. Put the dough back into the bowl, cover loosely with oiled clingfilm and leave in a warm place to rise for 1 hour or until doubled in size.

3 Tip the dough out on to a lightly floured surface, knead well then shape into a thick rope 73 cm (29 inches) long. Coil up loosely in the shape of a snail's shell and put into a 20 cm (8 inch) greased springform tin.

4 Cover loosely with oiled clingfilm and leave in a warm place to rise for 45 minutes or until the dough reaches the top of the tin.

5 Remove the clingfilm and brush with the egg yolk mixed with 1 tablespoon of water and sprinkle with the poppy seeds. Bake in a preheated oven, 200°C (400°F), Gas Mark 6, for 30 minutes until the bread is deep brown and sounds hollow when tapped with the fingertips. Check after 10 minutes and cover with foil if overbrowning.

6 Holding the tin with oven gloves, loosen the edges of the bread with a palette knife. Remove the outer ring of the tin and then the base. Transfer the bread to a wire rack to cool.

To make with a breadmaker

1 Lift the tin out of the bread machine, fit the kneader blade then add the measured cold water, beaten eggs, melted butter and honey. Spoon in the flour then add the salt. Make a slight dip in the centre of the flour and sprinkle in the yeast (see page 14).

2 Insert the tin into the bread machine. Shut the lid and set to dough or enriched dough. Press start.

3 At the end of the programme, lift the tin out of the machine, tip the dough out on to a lightly floured surface and continue as step 3, left.

Makes 1 large loaf

Tips This dough can be made into a single or double plait (see page 20) and served on the Sabbath or at other Jewish festivals. The three strands symbolize truth, peace and justice, while the poppy seeds represent the manna that fell from heaven.

As this bread contains fresh butter and an egg, do not use the delay timer facility.

3 yeast-free breads

Gingerbread

75 g (3 oz, ¼ cup plus
   2 tablespoons) dark muscovado
   sugar
100 g (3½ oz, 1 stick) butter
250 g (8 oz, 1½ cups) golden
   syrup
4 tablespoons (¼ cup) chunky
   marmalade
150 ml (¼ pint, ⅔ cups) milk
2 eggs
1 tablespoon chopped glacé or
   candied ginger, optional
300 g (10 oz, 2⅔ cups) plain or
   strong white flour
1½ teaspoons (1 teaspoon)
   baking powder
1 teaspoon bicarbonate of soda
1 teaspoon ground cinnamon or
   allspice
3 teaspoons ground ginger

To make by hand

1 Line and grease a deep 18 cm (7 inch) square tin.

2 Using a medium-sized saucepan, begin as steps 1 and 2, right.

3 Gradually pour the milk mixture, then the dry ingredients, into the pan. Stir thoroughly then pour the mixture into the prepared tin.

4 Bake in a preheated oven, 160°C (325°F), Gas Mark 3, for 45–55 minutes, or until a skewer inserted into the cake comes out cleanly.

5 Holding the tin with oven gloves, loosen the cake with a palette knife. Transfer to a wire rack and peel off the lining paper. Spread the top with the remaining marmalade.

Makes 1 large loaf

> **Tips** The top of the gingerbread can also be drizzled with glacé icing and sprinkled with a little extra chopped glacé ginger, instead of the marmalade for a festive alternative.
>
>   As bread machines differ, you may need to vary the cooking time by either stopping the machine before the programme has finished or by adding an extra 5–10 minutes. (Refer to your bread machine cookbook for details of how to do this.)

To make with a breadmaker

1 Put the sugar, butter, syrup and half the marmalade into a small saucepan and heat gently, stirring until the butter has just melted. Leave to cool slightly.

2 In a bowl, beat the milk, eggs and glacé ginger (if using) together. In another bowl, mix the flour, baking powder, bicarbonate of soda and spices.

3 Lift the tin out of the bread machine, fit the kneader blade then pour in the sugar mixture, milk mixture and the dry ingredients.

4 Insert the tin into the bread machine. Shut the lid and set to cake/quick bread, or follow your bread machine cookbook instructions if different (see page 12). Press start.

5 After 10 minutes or when the raisin beep sounds, open the lid and, using a plastic spatula, scrape down the sides of the tin to make sure there are no dry flour pockets. Allow the programme to continue.

6 As programme times vary from machine to machine, check the cake 15 minutes before the end of the programme. If golden brown and well risen, insert a skewer and if it comes out cleanly, the cake is ready. If not, leave until the programme ends then retest.

7 Lift the tin out of the machine with oven gloves. Loosen the cake with a plastic spatula then turn out on to a wire rack. Spread the top with the remaining marmalade.

Bara brith

This traditional Welsh fruit bread is a moist, cut-and-come-again cake that improves with keeping and is simply made with store cupboard ingredients. It is delicious thickly sliced and spread with butter.

125 g (4 oz, ½ cup) sultanas

125 g (4 oz, ½ cup) raisins

175 g (6 oz, ¾ cup) soft light brown sugar

300 ml (½ pint, 1¼ cups) hot strong tea

1 egg, beaten

275 g (9 oz, 2½ cups) self-raising flour

1 teaspoon bicarbonate of soda

1 teaspoon ground cinnamon

To make by hand

1 Put the dried fruit and sugar into a bowl and cover with the tea. Leave to soak for 4 hours or overnight.

2 Line the base and grease the base and sides of a deep 18 cm (7 inch) square cake tin.

3 Stir the beaten egg into the tea-soaked fruit. Sift in the flour, bicarbonate of soda and cinnamon and mix thoroughly. Spoon the mixture into the prepared tin and level the surface.

4 Bake in a preheated oven, 160°C (325°F), Gas Mark 3, for 55–60 minutes, until the bread is well risen and browned and a skewer inserted into the centre comes out cleanly.

5 Holding the tin with oven gloves, loosen the bread with a palette knife and transfer to a wire rack. Peel off the lining paper and leave to cool completely. Store in an airtight tin for up to 1 week.

> **Tip** The dried fruit can also be soaked in orange juice or milk instead of tea.

To make with a breadmaker

1 Prepare the fruit as step 1, left.

2 Lift the tin out of the bread machine, fit the kneader blade then add the tea-soaked fruit and beaten egg. Spoon in the flour then add the bicarbonate of soda and the cinnamon.

3 Insert the tin into the bread machine. Shut the lid and set to cake/quick bread or follow your bread machine cookbook instructions if different (see page 12). Press start.

4 After 10 minutes or when the raisin beep sounds, open the lid and, using a plastic spatula, scrape down the sides of the tin to make sure there are no dry flour pockets. Allow the programme to continue.

5 At the end of the programme, test the teabread with a skewer. If it comes out cleanly then it is ready. If not, set the machine to extra bake and cook for 10 more minutes, then retest. (Refer to your bread machine cookbook for more detail.)

6 Lift the tin out of the machine with oven gloves. Loosen the bread with a plastic spatula then turn out on to a wire rack and leave to cool. Store in an airtight tin for up to 1 week.

Makes 1 large loaf

Date and walnut soda bread

Traditionally made with buttermilk, which can be difficult to find, this modern version of soda bread is made with ordinary milk mixed with cream of tartar.

200 g (7 oz, 1¾ cups) strong wholemeal flour

275 g (9 oz, 2½ cups) plain flour

1 teaspoon bicarbonate of soda

½ teaspoon salt

125 g (4 oz, ½ cup) soft light brown sugar

250 ml (8 fl oz, 1 cup) milk

1 teaspoon cream of tartar

50 g (2 oz, ¼ cup) butter, melted

1 egg, beaten

75 g (3 oz, ¼ cup plus 2 tablespoons) walnut pieces

175 g (6 oz, ¾ cup) pitted dates, chopped

To make by hand

1 Put the flours, bicarbonate of soda, salt and sugar into a large bowl. Mix the milk and cream of tartar in a jug. Add the melted butter and egg to the flour with the walnuts and dates. Gradually mix in the milk to make a soft dough.

2 Tip out on to a lightly floured surface, knead briefly then pat into a 20 cm (8 inch) circle. Transfer to a greased baking sheet and make a cross cut on top of the dough.

3 Sprinkle with a little extra flour and bake immediately in a preheated oven, 220°C (425°F), Gas Mark 7, for 25–30 minutes until the bread is browned and sounds hollow when tapped with the fingertips.

4 Holding the sheet with oven gloves, loosen the bread with a palette knife and transfer to a wire rack to cool.

Makes 1 large loaf

Tip For a soft crust, wrap the hot bread in a clean tea towel and leave to cool.

To make with a breadmaker

1 Lift the tin out of the bread machine, fit the kneader blade then add the milk and mix with the cream of tartar. Add the melted butter and egg. Spoon in the flours, sugar, bicarbonate of soda and salt.

2 Insert the tin into the bread machine. Shut the lid and set to rapid/fastbake. Press start.

3 After 10 minutes, open the lid and, using a plastic spatula, scrape down the sides of the tin to make sure there are no dry flour pockets. Add the walnuts and dates and shut the lid. (This programme does not usually have a raisin beep facility.)

4 At the end of the programme, check the bread and programme for 15 minutes extra bake, if needed, to ensure the bread is cooked through. If your machine does not have this facility then either set for a full extra hour and turn off the machine manually (see pages 12–13), or lift the tin out of the machine, loosen the bread with a plastic spatula, turn out carefully on to a baking sheet and bake in a preheated oven, 220°C (425°F), Gas Mark 7, for 15 minutes until the top is firm and browned. Transfer to a wire rack to cool.

Lemon drizzle loaf

300 g (10 oz, 2⅔ cup)
   self-raising flour
2 teaspoons (1½ teaspoons)
   baking powder
150 g (5 oz, ⅔ cup) caster sugar
125 g (4 oz, ½ cup/1 stick)
   butter, melted
2 lemons, grated rind only
3 eggs, beaten
150 ml (¼ pint, ⅔ cup) milk

FOR THE SYRUP:
1 lemon, pared rind only
juice of 2 lemons
100 g (3½ oz, ⅓ cup plus 2
   tablespoons) caster sugar

To make by hand

1 Line the base and grease the base and sides of a deep 18 cm (7 inch) square cake tin.

2 Put the flour, baking powder and sugar into a large bowl. Add the melted butter and lemon rind then gradually mix in the beaten eggs and milk to make a soft spoonable mixture. Spoon into the prepared tin and level the surface.

3 Bake in a preheated oven, 160°C (325°F), Gas Mark 3, for 45–55 minutes or until golden brown, the top is cracked and a skewer inserted into the cake comes out cleanly.

4 To make the lemon syrup, see step 4, right.

5 Holding the tin with oven gloves, loosen the bread with a palette knife. Transfer to a wire rack set over a plate and peel off the lining paper.

6 Reheat the lemon syrup, if necessary. Make holes in the top of the cake with a skewer then pour over the lemon syrup and rind and leave to cool.

Makes 1 large loaf

To make with a breadmaker

1 Lift the tin out of the bread machine, fit the kneader blade then add the melted butter, eggs, milk, lemon rind and sugar. Spoon in the flour and baking powder.

2 Insert the tin into the bread machine. Shut the lid and set to cake/quick bread or follow your bread machine cookbook instructions if different (see page 12). Press start.

3 After 10 minutes or when the raisin beep sounds, open the lid and, using a plastic spatula, scrape down the sides of the tin to make sure there are no dry flour pockets. Allow the programme to continue.

4 Meanwhile, pare the lemon rind off the remaining lemon using a vegetable peeler. Cut the rind into thin strips and put it into a small saucepan with the lemon juice, the sugar and 4 tablespoons (¼ cup) of water. Simmer gently for 5 minutes until the lemon rind is clear and the liquid syrupy.

5 As programme times vary from machine to machine, check the bread 15 minutes before the end of the programme. If golden brown and well risen, insert a skewer and if it comes out cleanly then the bread is ready. If not, leave until the programme ends and then retest.

6 Lift the tin out of the machine with oven gloves. Loosen the bread with a plastic spatula and turn out on to a wire rack set over a plate.

7 Reheat the lemon syrup, if necessary. Make holes in the top of the cake with a skewer then pour over the syrup and lemon and leave to cool.

Banana, apricot and cherry teabread

Made with ripe bananas, this is a good recipe for using up those brown-speckled bananas in the fruit bowl and makes a good cake to pack in children's lunchboxes.

400 g (13 oz, 1½ cups) banana, about 3 small bananas, weighed with skins on

1 tablespoon lemon juice

300 g (10 oz, 2⅗ cups) self-raising flour

2 teaspoons (1½ teaspoons) baking powder

150 g (5 oz, ⅔ cup) caster sugar

125 g (4 oz, ½ cup/1 stick) butter, melted

2 eggs, beaten

125 g (4 oz, ½ cup) glacé cherries, roughly chopped

125 g (4 oz, ½ cup) ready-to-eat dried apricots, diced

To make by hand

1 Line the base and grease a deep 18 cm (7 inch) square cake tin.

2 Peel and mash the bananas with the lemon juice. Put the flour, baking powder and sugar into a large bowl then add the bananas and melted butter. Gradually beat in the eggs until smooth. Stir in the cherries and apricots. Spoon the mixture into the prepared tin and level the surface.

3 Bake in a preheated oven, 160°C (325°F), Gas Mark 3, for 45–55 minutes until well risen, the top has cracked and a skewer inserted into the loaf comes out cleanly.

4 Holding the tin with oven gloves, loosen the bread with a palette knife and transfer to a wire rack. Peel off the lining paper and leave to cool.

Makes 1 large loaf

To make with a breadmaker

1 Peel and mash the bananas with the lemon juice.

2 Lift the tin out of the bread machine, insert the kneader blade then add the bananas, eggs and melted butter. Spoon in the sugar then add the flour and baking powder.

3 Insert the tin into the bread machine. Shut the lid and set to cake/quick bread or follow your bread machine cookbook instructions, if different (see page 12). Press start.

4 After 10 minutes or when the raisin beep sounds, open the lid and, using a plastic spatula, scrape down the sides of the tin to make sure there are no dry flour pockets. Add the cherries and apricots and shut the lid. Allow the programme to continue.

5 As programme times vary from machine to machine, check the bread 15 minutes before the end of the programme. If golden brown and well risen, insert a skewer and if it comes out cleanly the bread is ready. If not, leave until the programme ends and then retest.

6 Lift the tin out of the machine with oven gloves. Loosen the bread with a plastic spatula, turn out on to a wire rack and leave to cool.

Chilli corn bread

1 tablespoon caster sugar

150 g (5 oz, ⅔ cup) yellow
cornmeal

250 g (8 oz, 2¼ cups) plain flour

3 teaspoons (2 teaspoons) baking
powder

1 teaspoon bicarbonate of soda

1 teaspoon salt

freshly ground black pepper

50 g (2 oz, ¼ cup) butter,
softened

50 g (2 oz, ¼ cup) Parmesan
cheese, grated

2 large whole dried chillies,
finely chopped

6 spring onions, finely chopped

2 eggs, beaten

150 g (5 oz, heaping ½ cup)
natural yogurt

300 ml (½ pint, 1¼ cups) milk

To make by hand

1 Line the base and grease the base and sides of a
deep 18 cm (7 inch) square cake tin.

2 Put the dry ingredients into a large bowl, add the
butter, cheese, chillies and onion. Whisk the eggs,
yogurt and milk together in a jug and add to the dry
ingredients and mix well. Spoon the mixture into the
prepared cake tin and level the surface.

3 Bake in a preheated oven, 160°C (325°F), Gas Mark
3, for 45–55 minutes or until well risen and golden
and the top has cracked slightly. Check the bread is
cooked by inserting a skewer into the centre. If it
comes out cleanly, the bread is ready.

4 Holding the tin with oven gloves, loosen the bread
with a palette knife. Transfer to a wire rack and peel
off the lining paper. Leave to cool.

To make with a breadmaker

1 Remove the tin from the bread machine, fit the
kneader blade then add all the ingredients except
the chillies and onions, in the order listed left.

2 Insert the tin into the bread machine. Shut the lid
and set to cake/quick bread or follow your bread
machine cookbook instructions if different (see
page 12). Press start.

3 After 10 minutes or when the raisin beep sounds,
open the lid and, using a plastic spatula, scrape
down the sides of the tin to make sure there are no
dry flour pockets. Add the chillies and onion and
shut the lid. Allow the programme to continue.

4 As programme times vary from machine to machine,
check the bread 15 minutes before the end of the
programme. If a skewer inserted into the bread
comes out cleanly, it is ready. If not, leave until the
programme ends and then retest.

5 Lift the tin out of the bread machine with oven
gloves, loosen the bread with a plastic spatula then
turn out on to a wire rack to cool.

Makes 1 large loaf

Tips If your loaf comes out with a pale top when
made in a bread machine, brush it with a little
butter and brown under the grill for 2–3 minutes.

As this bread contains fresh butter, cheese, eggs
and milk, do not use the delay timer facility.

gluten-free
breads

Spiced apple bread

500 g (1 lb, 4½ cups) gluten-free
   bread mix
2 tablespoons butter or margarine
2 tablespoons soft light brown
   sugar
1 teaspoon ground cinnamon
1½ teaspoons fast-action dried
   yeast
1 dessert apple, cored, coarsely
   grated
300 ml (½ pint, 1¼ cups) water

To make by hand

1 Line the base and grease a 1 kg (2 lb) loaf tin.

2 Put the bread mix into a large bowl, add the butter and rub in with the fingertips until the mixture resembles fine breadcrumbs. Stir in the sugar, cinnamon and yeast. Add the grated apple then gradually mix in enough warm water to make a smooth thick batter. Pour into the prepared tin and level the surface.

3 Leave to rise, uncovered, in a warm place for 45 minutes or until the mixture reaches the top of the tin.

4 Bake in a preheated oven, 200°C (400°F), Gas Mark 6, for 35–40 minutes until the bread is golden and sounds hollow when tapped with the fingertips. Check after 15 minutes and cover with foil if overbrowning.

5 Holding the tin with oven gloves, loosen the bread with a palette knife and transfer to a wire rack. Peel off the lining paper and leave to cool.

To make with a breadmaker

1 Lift the tin out of the bread machine, fit the kneader blade then add the measured cold water, butter, sugar and apple. Spoon in the bread mix and cinnamon. Make a slight dip in the centre of the flour and sprinkle in the yeast (see page 14).

2 Insert the tin into the bread machine. Shut the lid and set to basic white/large 750 g (1½ lb) loaf/bake and select the preferred crust setting, or follow the instructions in your bread machine cookbook for gluten-free breads. Press start.

3 At the end of the programme, lift the tin out of the machine with oven gloves. Loosen the bread with a plastic spatula then turn out on to a wire rack and leave to cool.

Makes 1 large loaf

Tips If the bread mix comes with a sachet of dried yeast, use the amount given in the ingredients list above.

   Always read labels on packet mixes carefully when making recipes for those following a special diet. It is important to be absolutely certain that they meet the necessary requirements and will not cause an allergic reaction.

Apricot, cranberry and pumpkin seed bread

500 g (1 lb, 4½ cups) gluten-free
    bread mix

2 tablespoons butter or
    margarine, softened

1½ teaspoons fast-action dried
    yeast

2 tablespoons thick set honey

1 egg, beaten

325 ml (11 fl oz, 1⅜ cups) water

25 g (1 oz, 2 tablespoons)
    pumpkin seeds

75 g (3 oz, ¼ cup plus
    2 tablespoons) ready-to-eat
    dried apricots, roughly chopped

75 g (3 oz, ¼ cup plus 2
    tablespoons) dried cranberries

extra pumpkin seeds, to decorate

To make by hand

1 Line the base and grease a 1 kg (2 lb) loaf tin.

2 Put the bread mix into a bowl, add the butter and rub in with fingertips until the mixture resembles fine breadcrumbs. Stir in the yeast, then add the honey and beaten egg. Gradually mix in enough warm water to make a thick batter. Stir in the pumpkin seeds, apricots and cranberries. Pour the mixture into the prepared tin. Level the surface and sprinkle with a few extra pumpkin seeds.

3 Leave to rise, uncovered, in a warm place for 45 minutes or until the mixture reaches just above the top of the tin.

4 Bake in a preheated oven, 200°C (400°F), Gas Mark 6, for 35–40 minutes until the bread is well risen, golden brown and sounds hollow when tapped with the fingertips. Check after 15 minutes and cover with foil if overbrowning.

5 Holding the tin with oven gloves, loosen the bread with a palette knife and transfer to a wire rack. Peel off the lining paper and leave to cool.

To make with a breadmaker

1 Lift the tin out of the bread machine, fit the kneader blade then add the measured cold water, beaten egg, butter and honey. Spoon in the pumpkin seeds and bread mix. Make a slight dip in the centre of the flour and sprinkle in the yeast (see page 14).

2 Insert the tin into the bread machine. Shut the lid and set to basic white/extra large 1 kg (2 lb)/ loaf/bake and select the preferred crust setting, or follow the instructions in your bread machine cookbook for gluten-free breads if different. Press start.

3 After 20 minutes or when the raisin beep sounds, add the apricots and cranberries. Check that they all mix in then shut the lid and allow the programme to continue. Sprinkle bread with pumpkin seeds just before baking begins.

4 At the end of the programme, lift the tin out of the machine with oven gloves. Loosen the bread with a plastic spatula then turn out on to a wire rack and leave to cool.

Makes 1 extra large loaf

> **Tip** Gluten-free breads dry out quickly so wrap them in clingfilm or foil as soon as they are cold.

Herb bread

Flecked with vibrant, fresh green mixed herbs, this tasty loaf is best served warm with soups or salads or toasted and topped with scrambled or poached eggs for a quick snack or lunch. For maximum flavour, use a mix of rosemary and sage with a little chopped chives or parsley.

150 g (5 oz, ⅔ cup) parsnip

200 g (7 oz, 1¾ cups) chick pea flour

300 g (10 oz, 2⅔ cups) gluten-free flour

1 teaspoon salt

1 teaspoon caster sugar

2½ teaspoons fast-action dried yeast

4 tablespoons (¼ cup) fresh chopped mixed herbs

2 tablespoons olive oil

400 ml (14 fl oz, 1¾ cups) warm water

To make by hand

1 Line the base and grease a 1 kg (2 lb) loaf tin. Then prepare and cook the parsnip, as step 1, right.

2 Put the flours into a large bowl then stir in the salt, sugar and yeast. Add the herbs and oil then gradually mix in enough warm water to make a thick batter. Pour into the prepared tin and level the surface.

3 Leave to rise, uncovered, in a warm place for 45 minutes or until the mixture reaches the top of the tin.

4 Bake in a preheated oven, 190°C (375°F), Gas Mark 5, for 30 minutes or until the bread is browned and sounds hollow when tapped with the fingertips.

5 Holding the tin with oven gloves, loosen the bread with a palette knife and transfer to a wire rack. Peel off the lining paper and leave to cool.

To make with a breadmaker

1 Peel and dice the parsnip. Cook in a saucepan of boiling water for 10 minutes then drain and mash.

2 Lift the tin out of the bread machine, fit the kneader blade then add the mashed parsnip, measured warm water, oil and chopped herbs. Spoon in the flours, salt and sugar. Make a slight dip in the centre of the flours then sprinkle in the dried yeast (see page 14).

3 Insert the tin into the bread machine. Shut the lid and set to rapid/fastbake. Press start.

4 At the end of the programme, lift the tin out of the machine with oven gloves. Loosen the bread with a plastic spatula and turn out on to a wire rack to cool.

Makes 1 large loaf

Tip If the bread looks pale when taken out of the bread machine, brush the top with a little melted butter or oil and grill for a few minutes until browned.

Quick cheesy corn bread

150 g (5 oz, ⅔ cup) fine cornmeal

125 g (4 oz, 1⅛ cups) chick pea flour

½ teaspoon salt

2½ teaspoons (1¾ teaspoons) wheat-free baking powder

50 g (2 oz, ¼ cup) Parmesan cheese, finely grated

50 g (2 oz, ¼ cup) butter, melted

2 eggs, beaten

300 ml (½ pint, 1¼ cups) milk

To make by hand

1 Line the base and grease a 1 kg (2 lb) loaf tin.

2 Put the cornmeal, chick pea flour, salt and baking powder into a large bowl. Add the grated Parmesan then the melted butter, beaten eggs and milk. Fork together to make a smooth batter. Pour the mixture into the prepared tin and level the surface.

3 Bake in a preheated oven, 160ºC (325ºF), Gas Mark 3, for 30–35 minutes until well risen, golden brown and the top is cracked and firm.

4 Leave in the tin for 10 minutes then loosen the bread with a palette knife. Transfer to a wire rack, peel off the lining paper and leave to cool.

To make in a breadmaker

1 Lift the tin out of the bread machine, fit the kneader blade then add the beaten eggs, butter, milk and Parmesan. Spoon in the cornmeal and chick pea flour then add the salt and baking powder.

2 Insert the tin into the bread machine, shut the lid and set to cake/quick bread, or follow the instructions in your bread machine cookbook for gluten-free/yeast-free breads if different. Press start.

3 At the end of the programme, lift the tin out of the machine with oven gloves. Loosen the bread with a plastic spatula and turn out on to a wire rack and leave to cool.

Makes 1 large loaf

Tips Ideally, the bread needs to be cooked on a programme that takes between 1 hour 40 minutes and 1 hour 50 minutes. On some machines the setting for this is 'cake', on others it is 'quick bread'. Read your bread machine cookbook and use the cycle that the manufacturer recommends.

As this bread contains fresh eggs and milk, do not use the delay timer facility.

Pumpkin and chilli bread

Gluten-free breads tend to be a little drier than breads made with wheat flour. To help compensate for this, a fiery mix of fried onions and diced pumpkin flecked with crushed cumin seeds and dried chilli flakes has been stirred into a mixed base of gluten-free flours.

2 tablespoons olive oil

1 small onion, finely chopped

125 g (4 oz, ½ cup) pumpkin or butternut squash, deseeded, peeled and finely diced

1 tablespoon cumin seeds, roughly crushed

¼ teaspoon dried chilli flakes

50 g (2 oz, ¼ cup) millet flakes

150 g (5 oz, 1⅓ cups) chick pea flour

200 g (7 oz, 1¾ cups) gluten-free flour

1 teaspoon salt

1 teaspoon sugar

2½ teaspoons fast-action dried yeast

350 ml (12 fl oz, 1½ cups) warm water

To make by hand

1 Line the base and grease a 1 kg (2 lb) loaf tin. Then prepare the pumpkin or squash as step 1, right.

2 Put the millet flakes, chick pea flour and gluten-free flour into a large bowl. Stir in the salt, sugar and yeast then add the spiced vegetable mix. Gradually mix in the warm water to make a thick batter. Pour the mixture into the prepared tin and level the surface.

3 Leave to rise, uncovered, in a warm place for 45 minutes or until the mixture just reaches the top of the tin.

4 Bake in a preheated oven, 190°C (375°F), Gas Mark 5, for 30 minutes or until the bread is browned and sounds hollow when tapped with the fingertips.

5 Holding the tin with oven gloves, loosen the bread with a palette knife and transfer to a wire rack. Peel off the lining paper and leave to cool.

To make with a breadmaker

1 Heat the oil in a frying pan, add the onion and pumpkin or butternut squash and fry gently for 10 minutes, stirring until lightly browned and cooked through. Sprinkle in the cumin seeds and chilli flakes and cook for 1 minute more.

2 Lift the tin out of the bread machine, fit the kneader blade then add the hot, fried vegetable mixture and the measured warm water. Spoon in the millet flakes, chick pea flour and gluten-free flour, salt and sugar. Make a slight dip in the centre of the flour and sprinkle in the yeast (see page 14).

3 Insert the tin into the bread machine. Shut the lid and set to rapid/fastbake. Press start.

4 At the end of the programme, lift the tin out of the machine with oven gloves. Loosen the bread with a plastic spatula and turn out on to a wire rack to cool.

Makes 1 large loaf

Index

Acknowledgements

Executive Editor: Nicola Hill
Executive Art Editor: Geoff Fennell
Editor: Rachel Lawrence
Designer: Claire Harvey
Production Controller: Louise Hall

Special Photography: Steven Conroy
Food Stylist: Sara Lewis

Special thanks to: Kenwood, Morphy Richards and Panasonic for loaning their bread machines for recipe testing and photography.